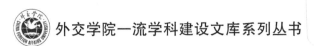
外交学院一流学科建设文库系列丛书

# 普遍管辖权的概念、逻辑和现状
## Universal Jurisdiction: Concept, Logic, and Reality

易显河　　王佳　等◎著

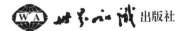
世界知识出版社

图书在版编目（CIP）数据

普遍管辖权的概念、逻辑和现状／易显河等著.

北京：世界知识出版社，2024.9

（外交学院一流学科建设文库系列丛书）

ISBN 978-7-5012-6746-0

Ⅰ.①普… Ⅱ.①易… Ⅲ.①管辖权—研究 Ⅳ.①D992

中国国家版本馆 CIP 数据核字（2024）第 028899 号

| | |
|---|---|
| 责任编辑 | 刘豫徽 |
| 责任出版 | 李　斌 |
| 责任校对 | 陈可望 |

| | |
|---|---|
| 书　　名 | 普遍管辖权的概念、逻辑和现状<br>Pubian Guanxiaquan de Gainian、Luoji he Xianzhuang |
| 作　　者 | 易显河　王佳　等 |
| 出版发行 | 世界知识出版社 |
| 地址邮编 | 北京市东城区干面胡同 51 号 （100010） |
| 经　　销 | 新华书店 |
| 网　　址 | www.ishizhi.cn |
| 电　　话 | 010-65233645（市场部） |
| 印　　刷 | 北京虎彩文化传播有限公司 |
| 开本印张 | 787 毫米×1092 毫米　1/16　13⅛印张 |
| 字　　数 | 160 千字 |
| 版次印次 | 2024 年 9 月第一版　2024 年 9 月第一次印刷 |
| 标准书号 | ISBN 978-7-5012-6746-0 |
| 定　　价 | 68.00 元 |

# 外交学院中央高校基本科研业务费专项资金项目

# 前 言

　　很久以来，人们对普遍管辖权的概念、范围和适用的认知存在很大的混乱。这种混乱在 2009 年以来联合国大会关于普遍管辖权范围和适用的辩论中体现得淋漓尽致。为了加深对普遍管辖权的理解，也多多少少怀有帮助人们对此概念进行正本清源的想法，我对该概念进行了认真的研究，并于 2011 年发表论文 "Universal Jurisdiction: Concept, Logic, and Reality"，[1] 即 "普遍管辖权的概念、逻辑和现状"，指出普遍管辖权的依据是其所针对的罪行是为国际社会所 "普遍关注"（universal concern）的罪行，所以可将此种类型的管辖权称为 "普遍关注" 型管辖权。即国家为惩治特定罪行，即使国家与犯罪人、受害者，或犯罪发生地没有具体的联系，也能够基于国际社会的 "普遍关注" 而行使普遍管辖权。真正或纯粹的普遍管辖权是一种仅以所涉罪行的受普遍关注性质为根据的管辖权。普遍管辖权的概念和逻辑是合乎情理的，因为每个国家均对受普遍关注之事拥有权益或发言权。普遍管辖权可成为国际体系维护

---

　　[1] Sienho Yee, "Universal Jurisdiction: Concept, Logic, and Reality," *Chinese Journal of International Law* 10, no. 3 (2011): 503–530, https://doi.org/10.1093/chinesejil/jmr041. 原文见本书附件；中文翻译版见本书第一章。

其权益、保护人权和对抗有罪不罚的强有力工具。然而，一国行使普遍管辖权可能会侵犯另一国的国家主权和主权平等，亦有可能滥用，从而破坏国际关系的稳定。这些正反两面以及其他方面的因素对国际法的形成过程产生了这样或那样的影响，以致迄今为止只有针对海盗罪的普遍管辖权已为国际法所接受。针对其他罪行的"纯粹的普遍关注型管辖权"（pure universal concern jurisdiction），目前还不存在。或许因为普遍管辖权一词的象征意义，以及人们喜欢标榜自己为拥护普遍管辖权以占领道德高地，常常把"普遍关注加某条件型管辖权"说成"普遍管辖权"。该论文进而对不同的涉"普遍关注"但不止于"普遍关注"型的管辖权进行分类并对其现状进行评估。鉴于这个分类和阐释对本人研究的统括性，在此较全面地援引如下。

（1）"纯粹的普遍关注型管辖权"（pure universal concern jurisdiction）。这一类型的管辖权是仅以罪行受普遍关注这一性质，再无他物，作为依据的一种管辖权主张。也就是"纯粹的普遍管辖权"（pure universal jurisdiction）或者"真正的普遍管辖权"（true universal jurisdiction）。如具合法地位，这种类型的管辖权可授予起诉国将犯罪嫌疑人引渡至该国进行审判的资格，如果其他条件获得满足的话。[2] 有时，该类型管辖权被称为"缺席的普遍管辖权"（universal jurisdiction in absentia），但该术语可能会和"缺席审判"

---

[2]　Cf. AIDP, 2009 Resolution on Universal Jurisdiction, para. Ⅱ（3）; but see IDI 2005 Resolution, para. 3（b）.

(trial in absentia) 相混淆，在此弃之不用。该类型管辖权包含以下两种情形：（i）一国单方主张纯粹的普遍管辖权；（ii）假设存在允许缔约国对非缔约国国民在缔约国以外的第三国领土上所犯的罪行主张纯粹的普遍管辖权的条约。后一种情形下，在涉及第三国问题上，条约体制整体并不比其某一特定缔约国拥有更大的权限，而授管辖权予条约体制缔约国的条约对于我们的评估意义不大。

（2）"普遍关注加现身型管辖权"（universal concern plus presence jurisdiction）。其可表述为：一国单方对现身于该国的非本国国民就其在本国以外的国家所犯之受普遍关注罪行行使管辖权的主张。此非严格意义上的普遍管辖权，因为犯罪嫌疑人的现身可能会使此种管辖权被认定为"属地管辖权"，而当现身持续至其归化取得国籍时，还大有可能被认定为"属人管辖权"。在犯罪嫌疑人的现身匆匆而过（如度周末）或只是短暂露面（如看病）的情况下，此时对管辖权的运用则会引起不同的界定：有人称之为普遍管辖权，有人则主张这是带有联系因素的管辖权。若控罪与起诉国之间缺乏联系因素是普遍管辖权的本质所在，那么犯罪嫌疑人在起诉国的短暂现身，可能不能否定此时主张的管辖权即普遍管辖权。然而，只要关于一国基于短暂现身主张管辖权的法律足够清晰，任何一个潜在的犯罪嫌疑人均有可能已有所察觉。如果此人继续前来该国，自动创设那样的联系因素，那么此时行使的管辖权可能会被认为不具有普遍性，无疑不是"纯粹的普遍管辖权"。

（3）"普遍关注加条约、现身型管辖权"（universal concern plus treaty and presence jurisdiction）。这种情形与第二种情形相近，但主张管辖权的依据，除上述第二种情形外，还增加了条约规定的义务或权利。可描述为：条约允许其缔约国针对现身于起诉国的第三国国民就其在第三国所犯的受普遍关注的罪行行使管辖权。

（4）"普遍关注加条约、现身并体制内属地或属人管辖权"（universal concern plus treaty, presence and intra-regime territoriality or nationality jurisdiction）。这与第三种情形相近，但适用范围较于第三种情形窄，增加了如下条件：犯罪嫌疑人或罪行必须与创设条约体制的某一条约缔约国之间存在领土、国籍或被害人国籍等联系因素。体制内属人联系因素可表述为：条约允许缔约国 A 对现身于其领土的缔约国 C 之国民 B，就其被控犯于非缔约国 D 的受普遍关注罪行进行起诉。体制内属地联系因素可表述为：条约允许缔约国 A 对现身于其领土的第三国（非条约缔约国）国民 B，就其被控犯于缔约国 C 领土上的受普遍关注罪行进行起诉。

上述情形中，只有第一种情形属于纯粹的或真正的普遍管辖权。第二种情形偏离了纯粹的普遍管辖权的轨道，但比其他情形更接近纯粹的普遍管辖权。第三、第四种情形并非真正意义上的普遍管辖权。第二种情形至第四种情形中，普遍关注（universal concern）在证明行使管辖权的正当性过程的角色，严格说来，是多余的。确切地说，若现身引发行使管辖权的条约义务，那么这样的管辖权可被认为，正如希金斯（Higgins）、科艾曼斯（Kooijmans）和伯索根尔（Buergenthal）等法官在"逮捕令案"（Arrest Warrant）中的联合个别意见[3]所言，"实际上是一种义务性的对人属地管辖权"（really an obligatory territorial jurisdiction over persons）。如果我们将这些情形称为"普遍管辖权"的话，那么"普遍管辖权"的价值就被稀释和贬损了。我们这是在玩文字游戏。[4]

鉴于这种局面，"荷花号案"论调（the *Lotus* dictum）及现身条件（the presence requirement）的潜在适用——尤其是关于其要求轻微、程序性观点，可能导致常需出访官员累遭起诉，具有重要意义而值得关注。另外，对普遍管辖权犯罪的宽泛解读，并借助于引渡条约要求引渡以宽泛解读来起诉的被告，值得注意和防范。

不过，国际法院在其 2002 年判决的"逮捕令案"中对普遍管辖权合法性问题保持引人注目的沉默，自那以来，追求"纯粹的普遍管辖权"的进程一直呈"下降趋势"。此后的下降趋势可能源于该案的审慎判决。该判决可被认为以一种巧妙的方式，帮助将某些

3　Arrest Warrant, Joint Separate Opinion of Judges Higgins, Kooijmans and Buergenthal, *ICJ Reports* 2002, pp. 74–75, para. 41.

4　上注 1，第一章，第 8 段。

冷静元素注入国际关系之中。随着比利时和西班牙现已通过收窄其法律适用范围从而放弃纯粹的普遍管辖权，追求纯粹的普遍管辖权的进程似乎成了一列正在行驶的没了机车头的列车。

2011 年论文发表后得到多方面的关注，有学者将它翻译成俄文发表，[5] 笔者也应邀就此文在 2013 年的美国国际法学会年会上作报告，[6] 该文为一管辖权研究手册收录，[7] 中文版也在 2019 年发表。[8] 当然，论文提出的观点、框架和对涉及普遍关注的管辖权的分类是否对国家实践产生实在的影响，不得而知，也无从考证。有意思的是，一名之前对"普遍管辖权"持十分宽泛解读意见的学者在 2015 年发表论文捍卫普遍管辖权时把他的文章题目定为《普遍管辖权并非在消失：从"全球强制者"型普遍管辖权（"global enforcer" universal jurisdiction）到"不提供安全港"型普遍管辖权（"no safe haven" universal jurisdiction）的转换》，[9] 这足以证明那列正在行驶的没了

---

5　Sienho Yee, Сиенхо Йии（Вухан, Китай）Универсальная юрисдикция: понятие, теория и практика, РОССИЙСКИЙ ЮРИДИЧЕСКИЙ ЖУРНАЛ, *Russian Juridical Journal* 85, no. 4（2012）: 7–31.

6　Sienho Yee, "A Call for a More Rigorous Assessment of Universal Jurisdiction," ASIL Proceedings（*American Society of International Law*）107（2013）: 242–245.

7　See Sienho Yee, "Universal Jurisdiction: Concept, Logic, and Reality," in Alexander Orakhelashvili（ed.）, *Research Handbook on Jurisdiction and Immunities in International Law*（Cheltenham: Edward Elgar Publishing, 2015）: 76–109.

8　参见易显河《普遍管辖权的概念、逻辑和现状》，易显书译，《国际法学刊》2019 年第 1 期，第 106—132 页。即本书第一章。

9　Máximo Langer, "Universal Jurisdiction Is Not Disappearing: The Shift from 'Global Enforcer' to 'No Safe Haven' Universal Jurisdiction," *Journal of International Criminal Justice* 13, no. 2（2015）: 245. 该作者曾在 2012 年发表长篇论文 Máximo Langer, "The Diplomacy of Universal Jurisdiction: The Political Branches and the Transnational Prosecution of International Crimes," *American Journal of International Law（AJIL）* 105, no. 1（2011）: 1–49。

机车头的列车的蒸汽越来越少了。[10]

同时，自 2009 年开始在联合国大会就普遍管辖权范围和适用的讨论洋洋洒洒，每年都在进行。[11] 2022 年 12 月，第 77 届联合国大会决定在第 79 届联合国大会成立一个第六委员会工作组，继续讨论普遍管辖权范围和适用，并邀请该工作组研讨普遍管辖权概念的相关要素。[12] 这个概念的未来如何，尚未知分晓。

在这个时间节点，我的上述论文发表 11 年多了。我和外交学院同事王佳副教授以及研究生董健宁、汪鑫宇、金凛、林芝羽、李介豪再次重拾这个话题，决定根据我 2011 年论文提出的观点、框架和对涉及普遍关注的管辖权的分类对国家实践进行梳理，并对国家实践的主要国别素材进行选编。本研究让我们感觉到，2011 年论文所提出的观点、框架和分类有助于加深对普遍管辖权的理解并对此概念进行正本清源，因此将该论文和相应材料一起合成本书出版，并附上 2011 年论文英文原文，以飨读者。

为了方便读者阅读和保证脚注之间相互援引及其与正文对照的准确性，本书每章的脚注重新连续编号。

易显河
外交学院
2023 年 8 月 27 日

---

10　只有阿根廷近年来好像在没有明确国内法基础的情况下展现了一些尚难以评估的激进趋势。见本书第 58—61、130—134 页。

11　从联合国大会第 64 届会议到最近的第 78 届会议，"普遍管辖权原则的范围和适用"不间断成为每届会议的议程项目（第六委员会的工作项目）。参见联合国大会第六委员会网，https://www.un.org/en/ga/sixth/78/universal_jurisdiction.shtml。

12　A/RES/77/111 (December 7, 2022).

# 目　录

# 普遍管辖权的概念、逻辑和现状*

易显河著　易显书译**

## 一、普遍管辖权的概念和逻辑

1. 近年来对普遍管辖权的援引，特别是针对非洲官员的时候，有被滥用之嫌，促使非洲国家联盟于 2009 年 2 月请求在第 63 届联合国大会会议议程内增列一项题为"普遍管辖原则的滥用"的临时项目。联大接受了该请求，从此，普遍管辖权在联大成为一个被热

　　* 本文系第 08&ZD055 号国家社会科学基金重大项目的组成部分，英文原文首次发表为"Universal Jurisdiction: Concept, Logic, and Reality," *Chinese Journal of International Law* 10, no. 3 (2011): 503-530。中文版首次见诸《国际法学刊》2019 年第 1 期，第 106—132 页。非常感谢威廉·沙巴斯（William Schabas）和《中国国际法论刊》审稿人对文稿所提的意见和评论。本文仅代表个人观点。本文于 2011 年 9 月 12 日完成。除非另有说明，本文引用的网络资料均截至该日。本文后记是在应爱德华·埃尔加出版社（Edward Elgar Publishing）重印本文时而作。可参见本书附件英文原文。作者特此向论文原文出版者 Chinese Journal of International Law 和牛津大学出版社，后记出版者 Elgar 和译文出版者《国际法学刊》和世界知识出版社鸣谢。
　　** 易显书，广东正大联合律师事务所合伙人，律师。

烈讨论的议题。2009 年秋天对该专题进行了辩论。联大接着要求各会员国政府提交有关国家实践的评论和信息。2010 年秋天联大再次对该专题进行了辩论。更多的信息得以挖掘，进一步的工作被列入 2011 年工作议程。[1]

2. 联合国会员国政府提交的评论和声明显示，人们对于普遍管辖权的概念、范围和适用的认知，极为混乱。为恰当理解普遍管辖权，重温一下对管辖权的通常理解将对我们有所帮助。通常，管辖权具有三个维度：立法管辖权、裁判管辖权和执行管辖权。国家刑事管辖权[2] 被认为一般以领土、国籍、受害人国籍，或国家重大利益的保护，来证明其正当性。有时，某一活动对一国产生的效果也被吸收进其中的一些原则。有时，条约可被认为是主张管辖权的一项独立依据，但未将正常的联系因素，例如领土，纳入其中的条约是否构成一项充分的依据，还是一个有争议的问题。每一项管辖依据都可能贯穿于管辖权的行使过程，从而导致产生一项类型不同的管辖权。以上列举的这些不同的依据于是引发不同类型的管辖权，一般被描述为属地管辖权、国籍管辖权、受害人国籍管辖权和保护管辖权。

---

1 有关该请求书和解释性备忘录，参见 A/63/237（February 3, 2009）and annex（"African Union memo"）。有关发展概览和文献资料，参见联合国大会第六委员会网 Sixth Committee（Legal）—64th session, *The Scope and Application of the Principle of Universal Jurisdiction（Agenda item 84）*, http://www. un. org/en/ga/sixth/64/UnivJur. shtml; Sixth Committee（Legal）—65th session, *The Scope and Application of the Principle of Universal Jurisdiction（Agenda item 86）*, http:/www. un. org/en/ga/sixth/65/ScopeAppUniJuri. shtml, 及"前言"注 11。

2 本章只探讨刑事普遍管辖权。

3. 考虑到这些因素以及目前并无一个国际规范化的普遍管辖权定义的事实，所提的很多定义和评论似乎将普遍管辖权表述为一种在控罪与企图行使管辖权的国家法律系统之间"缺乏"（absence）正常的管辖联系因素的管辖权。例如，（世界）国际法研究院（*Institut de Droit International*）在其 2005 年有关普遍管辖权的决议的第 1 段称：

> 刑事方面的普遍管辖权，是一种补充性的管辖依据，意指一国具有起诉和惩罚犯罪嫌疑人（如被定罪）的权能，不问被控罪行犯于何地，亦不问是否存在国际法承认的加害人国籍或被害人国籍，抑或其他管辖依据等任何联系因素。[3]

在（世界）国际法研究院上述项目的报告人看来，"正是控罪与起诉国家之间缺乏联系因素，'捕捉'了普遍管辖权的本质"。[4] 相似地，非盟—欧盟关于该专题的专家报告认为：

> 刑事普遍管辖权是一国对被控犯于他国领土，由非本

---

3　（世界）国际法研究院《关于灭绝种族罪、反人类罪和战争罪的刑事普遍管辖权决议》（2005 年克拉夫科通过，以下简称"国际法研究院决议"）第 1 段 "*Universal criminal jurisdiction with regard to the crime of genocide, crimes against humanity and war crimes*", para. 1, https://www.idi-iil.org/app/uploads/2017/06/2005_kra_03_en.pdf。

4　Christian Tomuschat, Rapporteur of the IDI Commission on Universal Criminal Jurisdiction, as quoted in IDI, *Annuaire de l'Institut de droit international* 71, no. Ⅱ（2006）: 257.

国国民针对非本国国民而犯，而又未对该主张管辖权的国家之重大利益造成威胁的罪行进行管辖的主张。换言之，普遍管辖权其实就是被控罪行犯下之时并不存在传统的属地、国籍、受害人国籍或保护原则等任何联系因素的情形下，一国对被控罪行进行起诉的权利要求。[5]

4. 然而，在"缺乏联系因素"的门面背后，搁着支持管辖权主张的基础，通常这样阐述：被控罪行损害了国际社会整体的基本利益，即违反国际强行法（jus cogens）或与之非常接近的某种法律，无论其实际称谓如何，如对世义务（obligations erga omnes，有时也说 erga omnes obligations）因此该罪行受国际社会整体的普遍关注（universal concern），而世界上的每个国家均对起诉犯罪者享有权益。[6] 另一相当重要的理由，在某些既定情况下，比在其他情况下，可能适用起来更加有效，即为确保某些特定的罪行受到惩罚，行使普遍管辖权是必要的。例如，海盗罪，通常犯于公海，如果不存在普遍管辖权，可能会逃脱惩罚。同样地，这些罪行，也许属稍有不同的一类，亦受普遍关注。作如是理解，将普遍管辖权表述为

---

5　AU-EU Expert Report, para. 8, http://ec. europa. eu/development/icenter/repository/troika_ua_ue_rapport_competence _universelle_EN. pdf.

6　See generally ALI, Restatement of the Law, Third, Foreign Relations Law of the United States（ALI, Restatement Third）, § 404 and the associated comments and notes; IDI Resolution, n. 3 above; and the IDI deliberations, IDI, 71（Ⅱ）Annuaire, n. 4 above, pp. 199−284; International Association of Penal Law（AIDP）, XVIIII Congress in 2009, Resolution on Universal Jurisdiction, http://www. penal. org/? page＝mainaidp&id_ rubrique＝24&id_ article＝95.

"普遍关注型管辖权"[7] 可能更为恰当，以和其他类型的管辖权，如"属地管辖权""国籍管辖权""国家利益保护管辖权"形成一定的对照。这些术语可令每一管辖权主张后面的依据立刻呈现在眼前。对普遍管辖权或普遍关注型管辖权的一种解释，或应为：它是以受普遍关注为依据，针对侵犯国际社会基本利益的罪行的国家管辖权的一种具体运用。[8]

5. 普遍关注型管辖权的逻辑理解起来并不费劲。受普遍关注作为国家行动的驱动力是被国际法院于 1970 年在著名的"巴塞罗那牵引力公司案"（Barcelona Traction）[9] 中提出来的。该案所解决的是外交保护问题，国际法院的著名判决因此不可被主张为直接的先例或是对普遍管辖权的直接支持。[10] 不过，判决关于这一问题的观点明显具有普遍适用性，可被认为是对普遍管辖权基本原理的具体阐释。在其中的第 33、第 34 段，国际法院分别指出：

原 33. 当一国许可外国投资和外国国民，不论自然人抑或法人，进入其领土时，其即承担为之提供法律保护和当予待遇的义务。然而，该义务既非绝对，亦非不受限

---

7　参见 ALI, Restatement Third, § 404：一国有权对被国际社会确认为受普遍关注之某些罪，如海盗、贩卖奴隶、攻击或劫持航空器、灭绝种族、战争罪行，或某些恐怖主义行为行使管辖权，对这些行为定罪量刑，即使缺乏第 402 条所列之任何管辖依据。

8　See ALI, ibid.

9　Case concerning the Barcelona Traction, Light and Power Company, Limited, Second Phase, Judgment, *ICJ Reports 1970*, p. 3.

10　See Rosalyn Higgins, *Problems and Process: International Law and How We Use It* ( Oxford: Clarendon Press, 1994) , pp. 57–58.

制。尤其应当在一国对国际社会整体的义务与在外交保护领域面对另一国的义务之间作本质的区分。正因其这一性质，前者事关所有国家。鉴于所涉权利的重要性，所有国家均可对其保护主张法律上的权益；此为对世义务（obligations *erga omnes*）。

原 34. 此等义务源自现代国际法，如禁止侵略和灭绝种族行为，亦源于有关基本人权的原则和规定，包括禁止奴隶制和种族歧视。与之相对应的所保护权利中，有的已构成一般国际法的主要内容（《关于〈防止及惩治灭绝种族罪公约〉保留问题的咨询意见》，载《国际法院 1951 年的报告》第 23 页），有的则由具有普遍或准普遍性质的国际法文件所赋。

6. 为落实这一理念，[11] 国际法委员会在《关于国家责任条款草案》（2001 年通过）第 48 条（"受害国以外的国家援引责任"）规定："1. 受害国以外的任何国家有权在下列情况下依照第 2 款对另一国援引责任：（a）被违背的义务是包括该国在内的一国家集团承担的，且为保护该集团的集体权益而确立的义务；或者（b）被违背的义务是对国际社会整体的义务。"[12]

7. 如此，总的来说，世上存在一些受普遍关注之事，而此等普

---

11　ILC Draft Articles on State Responsibility, art. 48, commentary, para. 8, in *ILC Report 2001*, A/56/10, 321.

12　*ILC Report 2001*, ibid. , p. 56.

遍关注足以构成国家采取一定行动的正当理由。本文要探讨的是，这一基本原理单独，或者这一基本原理加其他因素，或会如何证明一国行使普遍管辖权的正当性。但是，普遍管辖权并非受普遍关注的必然产物，即使这样的关注已经达到国际强行法要求的程度。[13] 仅有违反某一达到国际强行法地位的规则或违背对世权利义务（*erga omnes* rights or obligations，有时也说 rights or obligations *erga omnes*）的事实，并不导致产生国际法院或者别的国际法庭的管辖权，前者如国际法院在"刚果（金）诉卢旺达案"（*Democratic Republic of the Congo v Rwanda*）[14] 中所裁定，后者如国际法院在"东帝汶自决案"（East Timor）[15] 中所裁定。而单单同意（consent）则可使国际管辖权或国际法院（法庭）的管辖权得以创立。尽管我们在此所探讨的，某一国家法律系统行使管辖权的正当理由，在上述两案中未被提及，我们仍可得出相同的结论——违反具有国际强行法性质或对世性质的规范的行为本身并不导致产生国家法律系统的普遍管辖权。受普遍关注证明国家行使管辖权的正当性的潜能是否已经实现，或者达到何种程度，取决于哪些罪行可能被各国普遍认定为受普遍关注的罪行，以及此等受普遍关注是否事实上亦已被各国认定

13　See Paolo Picone, The Distinction between Jus Cogens and Obligations *Erga Omnes*, in Enzo Cannizzaro (ed.), *The Law of Treaties beyond the Vienna Convention* (Oxford: Oxford University Press, 2011), pp. 411, 421–422; but see generally Alexander Orakhelashvili, *Peremptory Norms in International Law* (Oxford: Oxford University Press, 2006).

14　Armed Activities on the Territory of the Congo (New Application: 2002) (*Democratic Republic of the Congo v Rwanda*), *ICJ Reports 2006*, p. 31, para. 64.

15　East Timor (*Portugal v Australia*), *ICJ Reports 1995*, p. 102, para. 29.

为足以构成行使这样的管辖权的正当理由。如何回答这些问题，将取决于国际法形成过程的现状。这是一个需要运用《国际法院规约》第38条所确立的标准法律渊源去评估的问题。那样的运用将在本文第二部分进行尝试。现在，让我们扼要思考一些一般性问题，这些问题能够构建起这样的一个评估框架，并帮助我们理解何者或已作为重要因素计入那一现状。

8. "普遍管辖权"这一术语已被各种不同的人士用来在不同的紧密或宽松程度上表示各种不同的意思，鉴于此，对可被视作普遍管辖权的情形，确切地说，或是与之类似的情形，按其类型作出一定的分类，将会对我们的探讨有所帮助。为把事情弄清楚，我们可按其"普遍性"强度的顺序，对这些类型作如下界定。

(1) "纯粹的普遍关注型管辖权"（pure universal concern jurisdiction）。这一类型的管辖权是仅以罪行受普遍关注这一性质，再无他物，作为依据的一种管辖权主张。也就是"纯粹的普遍管辖权"（pure universal jurisdiction）或者"真正的普遍管辖权"（true universal jurisdiction）。如具合法地位，这种类型的管辖权可授予起诉国将犯罪嫌疑人引渡至该国进行审判的资格，如果其他条件获得满足的话。[16] 有时，该类型管辖权被称为"缺席的普遍管辖权"（universal jurisdiction in absentia），但该术语可能会和"缺席审判"（trial in absentia）相混淆，在此弃之不用。该类型管辖权包含以下两种情形：（i）一国单方主张纯粹的普遍管辖权；（ii）假设存在允许缔约国对非缔约

---

16　Cf. AIDP, n. 6 above, para. II（3）; but see IDI 2005 Resolution, n. 3 above, para. 3（b）.

国国民在缔约国以外的第三国领土上所犯的罪行主张纯粹的普遍管辖权的条约。后一种情形下，在涉及第三国问题上，条约体制整体并不比其某一特定缔约国拥有更大的权限，而授管辖权予条约体制缔约国的条约对于本研究的评估意义不大。

（2）"普遍关注加现身型管辖权"（universal concern plus presence jurisdiction）。其可表述为：一国单方对现身于该国的非本国国民就其在本国以外的国家所犯之受普遍关注罪行行使管辖权的主张。此非严格意义上的普遍管辖权，因为犯罪嫌疑人的现身可能会使此种管辖权被认定为"属地管辖权"，而当现身持续至其归化取得国籍时，还大有可能被认定为"属人管辖权"。在犯罪嫌疑人的现身匆匆而过（如度周末）或只是短暂露面（如看病）的情况下，此时对管辖权的运用则会引起不同的界定：有人称之为普遍管辖权，有人则主张这是带有联系因素的管辖权。若控罪与起诉国之间缺乏联系因素是普遍管辖权的本质所在，那么犯罪嫌疑人在起诉国的短暂现身，可能不能否定此时主张的管辖权即普遍管辖权。然而，只要关于一国基于短暂现身主张管辖权的法律足够清晰，任何一个潜在的犯罪嫌疑人均有可能已有所察觉。如果此人继续前来该国，自动创设那样的联系因素，那么此时行使的管辖权可能会被认为不具有普遍性，无疑不是"纯粹的普遍管辖权"。

（3）"普遍关注加条约、现身型管辖权"（universal concern plus treaty and presence jurisdiction）。这种情形与情形（2）相近，但主张管辖权的依据，除上述第二种情形外，还增加了条约规定的义务或权利。可描述为：条约允许其缔约国针对现身于起诉国的第三国国民就其在第三国所犯的受普遍关注的罪行行使管辖权。

（4）"普遍关注加条约、现身并体制内属地或属人管辖权"（universal concern plus treaty，presence and intra-regime territoriality or nationality jurisdiction）。这与情形（3）相近，但适用范围较于情形（3）窄，增加了如下条件：犯罪嫌疑人或罪行必须与创设条约体制的某一条约缔约国之间存在领土、国籍或被害人国籍等联系因素。体制内属人联系因素可表述为：条约允许缔约国 A 对现身于其领土的缔约国 C 之国民 B，就其被控犯于非缔约国 D 的受普遍关注罪行进行起诉；体制内属地联系因素可表述为：条约允许缔约国 A 对现身于其领土的第三国（非条约缔约国）国民 B，就其被控犯于缔约国 C 领土上的受普遍关注罪行进行起诉。

上述情形中，只有情形（1）属于纯粹的或真正的普遍管辖权。情形（2）偏离了纯粹的普遍管辖权的轨道，但比其他情形更接近纯粹的普遍管辖权。情形（3）、情形（4）并非真正意义上的普遍管辖权。情形（2）至情形（4）中，普遍关注（universal concern）在证明行使管辖权的正当性过程的角色，严格说来，是多余的。确切地说，若现身引发行使管辖权的条约义务，那么这样的管辖权可被认为，正如希金斯、科艾曼斯、伯索根尔等法官在"逮捕令案"（Arrest Warrant）中的联合个别意见[17]所言，"实际上是一种义务性的

---

17　Arrest Warrant, Joint Separate Opinion of Judges Higgins, Kooijmans and Buergenthal, *ICJ Reports 2002*, pp. 74-75, para. 41.

对人属地管辖权"（really an obligatory territorial jurisdiction over persons）。如果我们将这些情形称为"普遍管辖权"的话，那么"普遍管辖权"的价值就被稀释和贬损了。我们这是在玩文字游戏。

9. 种种因素都可能贯穿于与普遍管辖权有关的国际法的生成过程中，导致出现目前对普遍管辖权的接受度现状。首先，普遍管辖权可被合理解释为：为保护国际体系的权益，包括保护人权和对抗有罪不罚，但由于我们经常号称的"国际社会"缺乏一个中央政府，故不得已而求其次，设立这样的一种制度安排性质的管辖权，运用国家法律系统并在此过程中去完成那一任务。从某种意义上说，国家法律系统可被认为处于一种执行"双重功能"（dédoublement fonctionnel）[18] 的状态。因此，期望保护国际体系的权益并对其维持和促进发挥作用的国家均有动力去促进普遍管辖权原则的确立和实施。其次，基于这一系统性考虑的普遍刑事管辖权对于另一系统性因素——国际强行法的执行或实施，似乎是必要的。否则，那一概念就没有实质意义了。那些认可国际强行法理念的国家可能同样具有乐于接受普遍管辖权的动力。

10. 另外，行使普遍管辖权可能会侵犯，或者说，至少有损国家主权和主权平等原则，也容易遭受政治滥用，包括出现在选择性诉讼中的差别待遇，从而破坏国际关系的稳定。正因如此，这种管

---

18  乔治斯·赛尔（Georges Scelle）提出这一术语。See Antonio Cassese, "Remarks on Scelle's Theory of 'Role Splitting' （dédoublement fonctionnel） in International Law," *European Journal of International Law*（*EJIL*）1, no. 1（1990）: 210.

辖权被认为是"危险的"。作如此描述的正是亨利·基辛格（Henry Kissinger）。[19] 当然，对普遍管辖权的任何行使，均最有可能对大国和强国有利。[20] 若如某些国家和"逮捕令案"专案法官范登韦恩加尔特（van den Wyngaert）所言，这是一个"事关面对那些滔天罪行之受害人的控诉，国际法要求或允许各国以国际社会的'代理人'身份去如何行动"的问题，[21] 人们可能会立刻质疑这样的代理人应否由一个特定的国家自己来"自我任命"。如果"荷花号案"论调（the *Lotus* dictum）得以取胜，这种担忧会进一步加大。[22] 再者，当各国行使普遍管辖权的尝试实际上可能被用来作交易时，普遍管辖权的政治性质将暴露无遗。面对北约总部迁离的威胁，比利时于 2003 年放弃其法律对普遍管辖权的强悍授权，就是一例。[23] 另一案例，至少在某种程度上让人蒙羞不已，在笔者看来，是在西班牙，当加尔松（Garzon）法官开始深入调查西班牙内战遗留下的不可告人的秘密的时候，西班牙于 2009 年废止其法律对普遍管辖权的

---

19　Henry Kissinger, "The Pitfalls of Universal Jurisdiction," *Foreign Affairs* (July–August 2001).

20　As pointed out by Shahabuddeen, in IDI Annuaire, n. 4 above, p. 228.

21　Arrest Warrant, diss. op., *ICJ Reports 2002*, p. 141, para. 5.

22　参见本章第三部分，第 44—49 段。

23　2003 年 8 月 5 日的《关于惩治严重违反国际人道法行为法》（Act on Grave Breaches of International Humanitarian Law）。正如由作出威胁的拉姆斯菲尔德所汇报：Donald Rumsfeld, *Known and Unknown: A Memoir* (New York: Sentinel, 2011), pp. 596–598。拉姆斯菲尔德汇报其与比利时国防部长德克雷姆进行了"直率和全面"的交流；交流中，拉姆斯菲尔德明确指出，在东道国怀有敌意的情形下，北约将考虑再次将其总部迁离，就像曾经迁离法国一样。"如果比利时政府不迅速改变其立场，美国对北约总部新址建设的支持将顷刻人间蒸发。"出处同前，第 598 页。拉姆斯菲尔德似乎对此很得意："一个生于芝加哥的美国人和欧洲外交使团成员之间的风格差异，在会谈中暴露无遗。从他的神态看，我想他完全明白我的意思。会谈后两个月内，比利时政府即废止其相关法律。"出处同前，第 598 页。

强悍授权。[24]

11. 显然，普遍管辖权的机制将给国家和解努力，如南非后种族隔离时代和一些拉丁美洲国家的尝试，带来严峻的挑战。如基辛格所言：

> 犯下战争罪行和系统地侵犯人权者应当承担责任，这是一个重要的原则。但一个争取就野蛮历史问题达成妥协的国家的法律、国内和平，以及代议制政府的巩固，也享有权利要求。惩罚的本能必须，如同每一个民主政治架构一样，与包括对民主的生存和壮大起关键作用的其他要素在内的分权制衡制度相联系。[25]

12. 这些因素以及未在此讨论的其他因素[26]无疑在国际法的形成过程中留下了深刻的印记，导致出现我们将在以下章节中进行讨论

---

24　参见 Jaclyn Belczyk, "Spain Parliament Passes Law Limiting Reach of Universal Jurisdiction Statute," October 16, 2009, http://jurist. law. pitt. edu/paperchase/2009/10/spain- parliamentpasses-law-limiting. php; Daniel Woolls, "Baltasar Garzon, Spanish Super Judge, Suspended Over Alleged Abuse," AP News, May 14, 2010, http://www. huffingtonpost. com/2010/05/14/baltasar-garzon-spanish-s _ n _ 576 872. html; Scott Horton, *The Poet, the Judge, and the Falangists*, http://harpers. org/archive/2010/04/hbc-90006895。

25　Kissinger, n. 19, above.

26　See generally Luc Reydams, "The Rise and Fall of Universal Jurisdiction, Leuven Centre for Global Governance Studies," Working Paper No. 37, January 2010, http://ghum. kuleuven. be/ggs/publications/working_papers/new _ series/wp31-40/wp37. pdf ("Leuven Working Paper"); papers by George Fletcher, Louise Arbour, Antonio Cassese and Georges Abi-Saab, *Journal International Criminal Justice* 1, no. 3 (2003): 580-602.

的当前局面。

# 二、国际法中的普遍管辖权现状

13. 尽管普遍管辖权的理念听起来似乎很有道理，其逻辑似乎也有说服力，但我们一定不能忘记一个智训："法律的生命在于经验而非逻辑。"[27] 从国际关系的经历和现状看，针对海盗罪以外的其他罪行的普遍管辖权还没有被确立为国际法的一部分。

14. 相关主要官方文件的表述不够清晰，现有对其的分析也不够客观和严谨，这给我们探讨国际法中的普遍管辖权带来了障碍。表示支持普遍管辖权的过甚其词的评论经常可在不同作者的作品中找出。不过，如果考查得更加严密和细致一些，可能会得出不同的结论。[28] 鉴于人们对依照国际法对海盗罪行使普遍管辖权的合法性不存争议，本文将不对海盗罪进行分析。

## （一）条约实践

15. 针对受普遍关注罪行行使管辖权的条约不胜枚举，这给任

---

27　O. W. Holmes, *The Common Law* (1886), p. 1.

28　See generally, Luc Reydams, Leuven Working Paper, above 26; Luc Reydams, *Universal Jurisdiction: International and Municipal Legal Perspectives* ( Oxford: Oxford University Press, 2003 ); William Schabas, Foreword, ibid.; Zdzislaw Galicki, ILC Special Rapporteur, *Fourth Report on the Obligation to Extradite or Prosecute* ( aut dedere aut judicare ), A/CN. 4/648, May 31, 2011, http://daccess-dds-ny. un. org/doc/UNDOC/GEN/N1/358/84/PDF/N1135884. pdf. 有关对普遍管辖权在国际法中的地位的一个乐观评估，参见 V. D. Degan and Vesna Baric Punda, "Universal Jurisdiction: An Option or a Legal Obligation for States, " *International Law Review of Wuhan University* 13 ( 2010 ): 66-92.

何一个苦心孤诣的学者均提出了一个艰巨的任务。关于这些条约应当如何归类和评价的文献也汗牛充栋。[29] 确切地说，围绕何者构成普遍管辖权的争论使这一任务变得更加困难。笔者首先将简要总结一下针对这些条约的现行讨论（同时附带笔者自己的评论），接着将根据笔者的分类总结对这些条约进行归整。

（Ⅰ）对条约实践的现行评价

16. 头号和最有资格成为纯粹的普遍管辖权适用对象的现代犯罪大概是灭绝种族罪。相信笔者无须再为证明灭绝种族罪的受普遍关注性质浪费笔墨。然而，针对该罪适用普遍管辖权的提议曾两次被专门辩论并遭拒。第一次是在联合国大会起草和通过第 96（Ⅰ）号决议时（1946），另一次则是起草和通过《防止及惩治灭绝种族罪公约》时（1948）。[30] 该公约的第六条最终采纳依赖于传统的属地管辖和一个有待成立的国际法庭。

17. 那些声称已发现普遍管辖权存在的人士常常利用大量条约中的各种"引渡或起诉"（extradite or prosecute）条款来作为证据，主张这些条款体现了普遍管辖权的存在。这种主张经不起条约实践的认真检验：虽然所针对罪行的受普遍关注性质可能对这些条约的缔结起到了促进作用（很少有人不同意这一观点），但行使管辖权可能还有其他依据。"引渡或起诉"是行使管辖权的一种方式，并

---

29　See ILC Special Rapporteur, ibid.; Reydams, ibid.

30　See William Schabas, *Genocide in International Law: The Crime of Crimes*, 2nd ed.（Cambridge: Cambridge University Press, 2009）, pp. 49-116, 411-416.

非管辖权本身。[31] 行使管辖权的方式方法不应与管辖权本身混为一谈。"引渡或起诉"义务可能适用于基于任何因素的管辖权，或者是领土、国籍、国家重大利益，或者甚至是受普遍关注。因此，采取这一方式行使管辖权，并不表示这一方式本身必然导致产生某一特定的管辖权或管辖权基础，此时所有可能被运用的管辖权或管辖权基础均有产生的可能。

18. 关键点是识别这一方式（"引渡或起诉"）被运用来实施何种管辖权。这显示，并无条约明确规定使用"引渡或起诉"原则实施纯粹的普遍管辖权，因此没有明确的条约实践支持纯粹的普遍管辖权理念。在"逮捕令案"中，在指责多数意见不处理管辖权问题，并对几份重要的条约进行考察后，希金斯、科艾曼斯和伯索根尔法官在其联合个别意见第 41 段[32]得出结论称：

> 原 41. 这些条约的缔约国就管辖权的依据以及就采取必要措施确立这样的管辖权的义务达成一致。这些具体的依据取决于犯罪者国籍、有关的船舶、航空器国籍或受害人国籍等联系因素。例如参见《海牙公约》第 4 条第（1）款，《东京公约》第 3 条第（1）款，《反对劫持人质国际公约》第 5 条，《禁止酷刑公约》第 5 条。这些被描述为基于充分的条约基础的域外管辖权可能更加准确。但除此

---

[31] 有关这一差别的另一阐述，参见 *AU-EU Expert Report*, n. 5 above, para. 11。

[32] Joint Separate Opinion, n. 17 above, pp. 74-75, para. 41.

之外，还存在一些类似的规定，根据这些规定，缔约国在行使管辖权过程中发现这些罪行的犯罪嫌疑人时，有义务将其起诉或引渡。由于措辞宽松，后者达到了可被视为"普遍管辖权"的程度，尽管其实际上只是一种义务性的对人属地管辖权，即使该人的罪行犯于他处。

19. 在这样的一种情形，即犯罪嫌疑人仅现身于起诉国，而起诉国拒绝对其引渡，其受争议的行为又与起诉国之间并无联系因素，构成行使管辖权之正当理由的情况下，那么，这种情形仅仅是如希金斯等法官在前所述，还是事实上构成了普遍管辖权或者限制性的普遍管辖权，似乎还是一个悬而未决的问题。控罪发生后的这一"仅有现身"情形明显就是《日内瓦公约》（1949）关于遏制"严重破坏"公约行为的相关规定（《第一公约》第49条，[33]《第二公约》第50条，《第三公约》第129条，《第一附加议定书》第85条）所关注的情形。国际红十字会在各种不同的声明中均明显将这

---

33　该条相关部分规定：各缔约国担任制定必要之立法，俾对于本身犯有或令人犯有下条所列之严重破坏本公约之行为之人，处以有效之刑事制裁。各缔约国有义务搜捕被控为曾犯或曾令人犯此种严重破坏本公约行为之人，并应将此种人，不分国籍，送交各该国法庭。该国亦得于自愿时，并依其立法之规定，将此种人送交另一有关之缔约国审判，但以该缔约国能指出案情显然者为限。"搜捕"一词可被恰当地解释为"搜捕据传现身于其领土之人"。See Jean S. Pictet's commentary, "Convention（Ⅰ）for the Amelioration of the Condition of the Wounded and Sick in Armed Forces in the Field, Geneva," August 12, 1949（1952）: 365 - 366, http://www.icrc.org/ihl.nsf/COM/365-570060?OpenDocument.

一体制视作普遍管辖权的一种。[34] 国际红十字会关于习惯国际人道法的研究似乎也如此认为。[35] 在其他场合下，[36] 或以其他的方式，[37] 某些政府似乎也将这种情形视作"普遍管辖权"。

20. 这一观点明显也得到了（世界）国际法研究院的背书。在关于普遍管辖权议题的辩论过程中，（世界）国际法研究院的项目报告人强调把罪行与起诉国之间缺乏联系因素作为查明普遍管辖权的标准。[38] 这一"仅有现身"情形明显不被认为构成这样的一个联系因素。2005 年的（世界）国际法研究院决议的最终文本在第 2 段声称：

> 普遍管辖权主要基于习惯国际法。其亦可依调整缔约国之间关系的多边条约，尤其根据条约中规定在自己领土上发现犯罪嫌疑人的缔约国有义务将犯罪嫌疑人引渡或审判的条款而确立。[39]

---

34 《国际红十字会代表在联合国第六委员会的发言》，A/C. 6/65/SR. 12, October 15, 2010, 6, para. 42；《国际红十字会 2003 年 8 月 27 日关于〈日内瓦禁止生物和有毒武器公约〉缔约国专家会议第一会议（2003 年 8 月 18—29 日）的官方声明》，http://www.icrc.org/web/eng/siteeng 0.nsf/htmlall/5qkdpf ["应当记起的是，各国已被要求对日内瓦公约（1949）及第一议定书（1977）的'严重破约'行为行使普遍管辖权，这些行为只针对武装冲突中受保护人员的故意杀害、酷刑和不人道待遇，包括生物学实验、对平民人群和个人身体的严重伤害，使用生物武器等同于这样的'严重破约'行为，因此需要对其主张普遍管辖权"]。

35 See Jean-Marie Henckaerts & Louise Doswald-Beck (eds.), *1 Customary International Humanitarian Law (ICRC Study)*, Rule 157 and the associated support in Vol. 2.

36 参见成员国政府就《反酷刑公约》议案所阐述的观点：E/CN. 4/1983/63, paras. 22 & 23。

37 一般参见英国政府的观点，引述于 Ian Brownlie, *Principles of Public International Law*, 7th ed. (Oxford: Oxford University Press, 2008), pp. 305–306。

38 IDI Annuaire, n. 4 above, p. 257; p. 261 (Rapporteur).

39 IDI Resolution, n. 3 above.

上述第二句在包括希金斯和阿比萨布（Abi-Saab）在内的部分成员的反对声中被通过。[40]

21. 再者，一些条约要求控罪与一特定条约的某些缔约国之间存在重要的联系因素，如领土或者国籍，这些与条约体制整体之间的联系因素明显否定"仅有现身"情形属于真正意义上的普遍管辖权的运用。此即上文重点描述之"普遍关注加条约、现身并体制内属地或属人型管辖权"。这一情形属于典型的条约体制内部的协作事务，其意指，至少条约体制内的某一缔约国可以基于某一传统标准合法地行使管辖权，起诉国不过是在代替另一缔约国履行职责，不管该缔约国出于何种原因没有履行职责（如无能力管辖或不愿管辖）。这一条约体制实质上允许缔约国分享其传统的管辖权力，或者允许某一缔约国行使另一缔约国的管辖权。《日内瓦公约》（*Geneva Conventions*）则使用宽松的措辞（"不问国籍出处"）来描述"引渡或起诉"的义务，但那些公约的适用可能——尽管不是很清晰——要求控罪犯于公约某一缔约国的领土，因此要求控罪至少与被援引条约的某一缔约国之间存在基层的联系因素如国籍、领土、受害人国籍，或者重大利益。无论如何，此后，有关公约，例如《禁止酷刑和其他残忍、不人道或有辱人格的待遇或处罚公约》（1984），对此的规定已更加清晰，其规定：犯罪嫌疑人"仅有现身"于某一缔约国的领土具有第二层级的性质；欲将犯罪嫌疑人置于一定的程

---

40　IDI, 71（Ⅱ）Annuaire, n. 4 above, pp. 209–210（Abi-Saab）; p. 257（Higgins）.

序，控罪或犯罪嫌疑人必须与公约的某一缔约国之间具有某一基层的联系因素，如领土、国籍。这至少是对《禁止酷刑公约》第5条的一种合理解读。该条规定如下：

第5条

1. 每一缔约国均应尽可能采取各种措施，以确保在下列情况下，对第4条所述之罪行行使管辖权：

（a）被控罪行发生于其管辖的任何领土内，或者发生在注册于该国的船舶或航空器上；

（b）被控犯罪嫌疑人为该国国民；

（c）受害人为该国国民，而该国认为适宜管辖。

2. 每一缔约国亦应尽可能采取各种措施，确保在下述情况下，对此种罪行行使管辖权：被控罪行发生于该国管辖的任何领土内，而该国不依第8条规定将被控犯罪嫌疑人引渡至本条第1款所述之任何国家。

3. 本公约不排除依国内法行使的任何刑事管辖权。

本条第1款规定以领土、国籍，或受害人国籍为基础确立管辖权的义务。第2款规定在犯罪嫌疑人没有被"引渡至本条第1款所述之任何国家"时对其起诉的义务。对这一规定的解读之一是：适用第2款的前提是第1款必须已具潜在适用性，但被请求国不愿引渡被控犯罪嫌疑人。也就是说，犯罪嫌疑人或者被控罪行必须与某一缔约国（第 1 款所述之每一缔约国，只针对缔约国）之间存在基层的联系因素——领土、国籍或受害人国籍——以确立这一潜在适用性。如此解读，第 5 条第 2 款则不处理本条约体制本职之外的事务。

22. 对这一条约体制作更进一步和更清晰阐述的是《国际刑事法院罗马规约》。该规约第 12 条规定国际刑事法院——一个可被视为缔约国家的合作组织——以被控罪行与缔约国之间的领土联系因素，或被控犯罪嫌疑人与缔约国之间的国籍联系因素为基础取得管辖权。

23. 有人或会争辩说，对《日内瓦第一公约》第 49 条和日内瓦其他公约相应条款以及《禁止酷刑公约》第 5 条第 2 款，可能还有一个可供选择的更为宽松的解读版本。这一可供选择的解读版本或不要求以犯罪嫌疑人或控罪与缔约国之间存在基层的联系因素作为触发"引渡或起诉"义务的条件。确实，《日内瓦第一公约》的措辞如此宽松，以致作出这种版本解读是有可能的。再者，对于《禁止酷刑公约》第 5 条第 2 款，人们可以设想这样的一种解读：无论何种原因，无论何时，只要犯罪嫌疑人不被引渡至任何缔约国，第 2 款即可援引。根据这一解读，第 1 款是否具有潜在适用性并不重要，不过，如果不可适用，这也将是因为被控在第三国针对第三国的国民并在第三国领土犯下控罪的犯罪嫌疑人是第三国的国民，而又没有被引渡至任何缔约国。不过，这种解读似乎使第 5 条第 2 款的部分措辞变得累赘和不自然。如果选择接受这一版本，那么这一情形该属上文重点描述的"普遍关注加现身型管辖权"。

24. 这一情形的其他实例包括《关于制止非法劫持航空器的公约》(1970《海牙公约》) 第 4 条第 2 款[41]和《禁止并惩治种族隔离罪行国际公约》(1973) 第 5 条。[42] 两者皆可被理解为授权对现身于起诉国（被援引公约的缔约国）的犯罪嫌疑人就其发生于第三国的控罪行使管辖权。我们不能确定这一解读是否准确，这些规定被如此适用的记录，不管行政上的还是司法上的，似乎还不存在。

25. 然而，即便是这一"普遍关注加条约、现身型管辖权"也不是真正的或纯粹的普遍管辖权，因为它以条约许可或义务以及犯

---

41　See Joint Separate Opinion, *ICJ Reports 2002*, 73, para. 35; President Guillaume, Separate Opinion, ibid. , 38, para. 7. 纪尧姆（Guillaume）院长个别意见强调确立管辖权的义务，于是"起诉的义务不再以管辖权的存在为条件，而是管辖权本身必须被确立，以使起诉成为可能"。其似乎将此称为"强制性普遍管辖权，尽管具有附属性"。其认为《关于制止非法劫持航空器的公约》第 4 条第 2 款是这方面的先驱。如果确立管辖权的义务不能被认为是"引渡或起诉"这一术语的逻辑引申或已包含在这一术语之内，那么人们可能赞同这一强调内容。起诉意味着起诉的必备条件的存在，即管辖权的确立。不管怎样，采取必要措施遏制犯罪的总体承诺应已包含这一义务。这是对《日内瓦第一公约》(1949) 措辞宽松的第 49 条，尤其是第 1 款，以及其他《日内瓦公约》的相应条款的理解。再者，《关于制止非法劫持航空器的公约》(1970) 第 4 条第 2 款明文规定以犯罪嫌疑人在缔约国的现身为条件，而《日内瓦第一公约》(1949) 第 49 条亦被解释为要求相同的条件。也就是说，1970 年《海牙公约》可能并非第一份规定以此作为确立管辖权条件的文件。

42　《禁止并惩治种族隔离罪行国际公约》(1973) 第 5 条规定："被控犯有本公约第二条所列举的行为的人，得由对被告取得管辖权的本公约任何一个缔约国的主管法庭，或对那些已接受其管辖权的缔约国具有管辖权的一个国际刑事法庭审判。""对被告取得管辖权"的表述不是很清晰，不过在笔者看来，其意明显是指被告的现身。从公约通过当时的环境和流行的外交气候看，该公约显得颇为特别。参见约翰·迪加尔的评论，John Dugard, "UN Legal Counsel delivers an address to diplomats and practitioners at the 41st Annual International Humanitarian Law Seminar," UN, p. 2, https://legal. un. org/avl/pdf/ha/cspca/cspca_e. pdf。他说："《禁止并惩治种族隔离罪行国际公约》允许缔约国对非缔约国国民就其被控犯于非缔约国领土上的罪行进行起诉，如果被告人身处某一缔约国的管控之下（公约第 4、第 5 条）……尽管种族隔离在南非存在已久，但没有人因种族隔离罪被起诉。自从公约通过以来，还没有人因该罪被起诉"。但雷丹姆斯（Reydams）似乎将公约第 5 条阐述为授予普遍管辖权（cf. Leuven Working Paper, n. 26 above, p. 18)。

罪嫌疑人现身作为行使管辖权的条件。只有当条约宣布授权其缔约国对与条约的任何缔约国之间无任何联系因素的罪行和犯罪嫌疑人行使管辖权的时候，人们才有可能看到纯粹的普遍管辖权。例如，假如 1970 年《海牙公约》授权起诉国（公约缔约国）对未现身于该公约之缔约国以外的第三国国民就发生于第三国的控罪行使管辖权，这就创作了一个纯粹的普遍管辖权剧本。然而，要找出这样的条约并非一件轻松的事情，不过，笔者也还没有对此作透彻的研究。已对普遍管辖权进行深入研究的"逮捕令案"中的法官们（尤其是那些就普遍管辖权问题发表意见的法官）和各类学者也还没有宣称找到了这样的一份条约。

26. 某些条约的条款的措辞可能会给人带来这样的印象或论调：该条约以某种方式默认普遍管辖权。例如，《关于发生武装冲突时保护文化财产公约第二议定书》（1999）在 16 条第 2 款第（a）项[43]规定，该议定书"不妨碍依据有关国内或国际法承担个人的刑事责任和行使管辖权，也不影响根据国际习惯法行使管辖权"。国际红十字会的习惯国际法专家持这样的观点：

> 《关于发生武装冲突时保护文化财产公约第二议定书》
> （1999）规定其"不影响根据国际习惯法行使管辖权"，这
> 是缔约代表们在缔结议定书的过程中提出来的，旨在赋权

---

43　参见联合国教科文组织网，http://portal. unesco. org/en/ev. php-URL_ID=15207&URL_DO=DO_TOPIC&URL_SECTION=201. html。

缔约国援引这一规定来授权其国内法庭对战争罪行行使普遍管辖权。[44]

但专家们并未提出来自起草历史方面的证据。

27. 最好不要对这一规定作如是解读；将之理解为一项防止对上述第二议定书第 16 条作反向解释（该规定禁止行使未在本条列出的其他类型管辖权）的规定，更为恰当。如果将之理解为这是在支持行使某一特定类型管辖权譬如普遍管辖权，则进行了一次大飞跃了。这一意思需要条约文本本身有肯定性的支持。这一更为恰当的解释得到类似解释——对《禁止酷刑公约》第 5 条第 3 款的通常解释——的支持。[45]

（Ⅱ）对条约实践的总结

28. 当我们试图提炼出任何习惯国际法规则的时候，我们并未能从凌乱的条约实践和学术讨论中获得多大的自信。那些被列入考虑范围的罪行之受普遍关注性质业已促进大量条约的缔结，不过，且不管我们如何谈论这些条约，牢记一条是明智的，那就是条约的权利或义务只适用于条约的缔约方，并取决于条约所定之一系列具体条件。[46] 然而，数据确实还没显示存有任何条约授权行使"纯粹的普遍关注型管辖权"的具体实例。某些条约授权或者可被解释为

---

44　*ICRC Study*, n. 35 above, vol. 1, 605, & n. 198.

45　See Joint Separate Opinion, n. 17 above, paras. 34, 38.

46　中国的声明和有关评论参见 https://www.un.org/en/ga/sixth/65/ScopeAppUniJuri_States Comments/China.pdf。中文本现在联合国网（原引用网址失效）；英译本现在联合国网，https://www.un.org/en/ga/sixth/65/ScopeAppUniJuri_StatesComments/China_E.pdf，有关评论，见第 6 段。

授权行使"普遍关注加条约加现身型管辖权"。实际上更多的条约授权行使"普遍关注加条约、现身并体制内属地或属人型管辖权"。但后两种类型皆不能被准确地称为"普遍管辖权"。

## （二）国际习惯法

29. 把目光转向普遍管辖权在国际习惯法中的地位，自然会令人想起根据《国际法院规约》第 38 条第 1 款（b）项规定去发掘出这样的一项规则：习惯国际法由经接受为法律（法律确信，*opinio juris*）之各国普遍实践所证明。

30. 从这个角度看，令人印象深刻的，是明确行使"纯粹的普遍关注"型管辖权的证据的匮乏，以及种种宣言和声明的宽松描述中所表现出来的貌似对"普遍管辖权"的广泛支持。若按表面价值去理解后者，似乎存在可被宽松用以针对灭绝种族罪、反人类罪和严重的战争罪行的普遍管辖权概念的法律确信。例如，早在 1971 年，联大的一项决议就措辞宽松，以和普遍管辖权的理念保持一致。在这项决议中，联大"申明各国在逮捕、引渡、审判和惩治战争罪犯和反人类罪犯过程中拒绝合作违背《联合国宪章》的宗旨和原则以及公认的国际法准则"。[47] 很多西方国家也发表声明支持普遍管辖权理念。[48] 非洲联盟在其关于在第 63 届联大会议议程增列有关普遍管辖权问题项目的请求书所附之备忘录中称，"普遍管辖权原

---

[47]  UNGA Res 2840 (1971).

[48]  有关进一步的信息，参见 *AU-EU Expert Report*, n. 5 above; *ICRC Study*, n. 35 above。

则已为国际法所充分确立"，"非盟尊重这一原则，该原则已被'蕴含'于《非洲联盟宪法性文件》第 4 条第（h）款"，但非盟对这一原则的范围和适用的含糊不清及其滥用感到担忧。[49] 美国法律学会，一个由法律专家组成的国家级学术团体，早在 1986 年就发现针对数种罪行的普遍管辖权存在于习惯国际法之中。[50]（世界）国际法研究院，一个由法律专家组成的世界级学术团体，也在 2005 年对普遍管辖权概念或原则给予支持。[51]

31. 无论如何，有关主张普遍管辖权的国家活动数据并未表明，除海盗罪的情形外，有足够的证据证实纯粹的普遍管辖权已被确立。这或多或少也是包括"逮捕令案"（2002 年）希金斯、科艾曼斯、伯索根尔法官和纪尧姆院长在内的西方法官的结论。希金斯、科艾曼斯和伯索根尔法官在"逮捕令案"中的联合个别意见[52]支持《奥本海国际法》（1996 年第 9 版，第 998 页）作者的见解，即：

> 虽然迄今为止还没有一项可被用来主张各国已被赋权，例如如同被赋权惩治海盗行为那样去惩治犯有反人类罪的外国国民之实在国际法一般规则，不过有明显的迹象

---

49　A/63/237, annex（Explanatory memorandum），para. 1. 不结盟运动国家的态度似乎更加模糊。参见 A/C. 6/64/SR. 12（November 25, 2009），paras. 20 - 21；A/C. 6/65/SR. 10（October 13, 2010），paras. 55-56。

50　ALI, Restatement of the Law, Third, the Foreign Relations of the United States, § 404 以及据此进行的评论和注释。有关原文复制在上注 7。

51　IDI Resolution, n. 3 above.

52　Joint Separate Opinion, n. 17 above, para. 52.

表明，带有此意的一项重大国际法原则在逐步发展当中。

如下文，尤其是第 34 段所述，此后的发展态势不仅没有加强，反而削弱了普遍管辖权的法律地位。从某种意义上说，当 2002 年"逮捕令案"判决之时，普遍管辖权的运气已达顶峰。

32. 尽管某些国家，例如英国，[53] 在其以手册形式展示的军事法律或条例中主张对战争罪行行使普遍管辖权，但这一主张似乎未在各国间引起普遍追随，也没有扩至其他罪行或其他控诉场合。实际上，甚至英国军事手册连说服英国自身的立法机构通过立法实施那一理念也还存在困难。[54] 而解决《罗马规约》实施的问题只得通过一个"聪明"的办法来解决。在对战争罪行行使普遍管辖权问题上，国际红十字会的研究似乎持一个更为宽松的观点。[55] 若对所示数据进行严格的分析，其判断可能得不到支持。

33. 一位评论家经过一番复杂的考察，认为包括《违反国际法的罪行法典》在内的德国立法已考虑到适用纯粹的普遍管辖权的可

53　British Manual of Military Law, III (1956), para. 637, as quoted in Rosalyn Higgins, *Problems and Process: International Law and How We Use It* (Oxford: Clarendon Press, 1994), pp. 59–60; see discussion of id., pp. 56–61; Ian Brownlie, *Principles of Public International Law*, 7th ed. (Oxford: Oxford University Press, 2008), pp. 305–306; UK Ministry of Defence, *The Manual of the Law of Armed Conflict* (Oxford: Oxford University Press, 2004), paras. 16. 30.

54　See Ian Brownlie, *Principles of Public International Law*, 7th ed. (Oxford: Oxford University Press, 2008), pp. 305–306; Rosalyn Higgins, *Problems and Process: International Law and How We Use It* (Oxford: Clarendon Press, 1994), pp. 59–61.

55　See *ICRC Study*, n. 35 above, Rule 157, 以及相关资料。

能性,[56] 但受种种条件限制。不过，时至今日，这一可能性仍然停留在可能性之上，因为还没有作出过这样的控诉。

34. 国家立法对纯粹的普遍管辖权的有限支持，近来被进一步削弱了。分别于 2003 年、2009 年，比利时[57]和西班牙[58]被普遍认为是曾经对主张纯粹的普遍管辖权有明确法律依据和曾经实际上行使过该管辖权的仅有的两个国家（不包括德国，因为德国立法模糊，亦无实施记录），修改其法律，规定行使管辖权应以与法院地国之间存在各种联系因素为条件。

35. 来自西方国家的有限案例几乎全部显示，普遍管辖权在被试图实施或实际实施时，被描述为"表明法院在援引普遍管辖权问题上大都表现谨慎"。[59] 此外，雷丹姆斯（Reydams）在 2010 年对这

---

56　参见其中的描述和分析：Luc Reydams, *Universal Jurisdiction* ( Oxford: Oxford University Press, 2003), pp. 141–147。

57　August 2003 Act on Grave Breaches of International Humanitarian Law ( Belgium). See Luc Reydams, "Belgium Reneges on Universality: 5 August 2003 Act on Grave Breaches of International Humanitarian Law," *Journal of International Criminal Justice* 1, no. 3 (2003): 679–689.

58　Ley Orga'nica 1/2009, de 3 de noviembre complementaria de la Ley de reforma de la legislación procesal para la implantacio'n de la nueva Oficina judicial, por la que se modifica la Ley Orga'nica 6/1985, de 1 de julio, del Poder Judicial ( http://noticias. juridicas. com/base _ datos/Admin/lo1-2009. html) ( Spain). 这一新法的实质，如西班牙政府代表在联大的发言所称 ( A/C. 6/65/SR. 11, October 13, 2010, 4, para. 21) ："法官只有在如下情况下才能对在世界上犯下严重罪行者进行起诉：没有国际法庭或第三国法庭已经启动针对这些人的诉讼程序，以及这些人现身于西班牙领土或者受害人为西班牙国民。"

59　See the analysis in the Joint Separate Opinion, n. 17 above, para. 21.

一情形描述如下：[60]

    总计起来，共有 24 名个人被澳大利亚、加拿大、德国、丹麦、比利时、英国、荷兰、芬兰、法国、西班牙和瑞士的法庭对其在国外所犯的"战争罪行"进行了审判。毫无例外地，这些被告均在法院地国取得了永久居留权——以难民、流亡者或者移民身份取得——且对被"遣返至其恶行发生国"实行抵制。大多数情况下，其他有关国家都默许，或者甚至支持起诉。此外，不要忽略一个事实，即这些案件中大部分均与发生在前南斯拉夫和卢旺达的暴行有关。专为这些国家而设的国际刑事特别法庭的检察官和联合国安理会鼓励所有国家在其领土上搜捕和审判（参看《日内瓦公约》义务）犯罪嫌疑人。最后，引渡常常成为不可能，不是法律上就是实践上不可行。

此外，明确主张普遍管辖权的罕有案例，还来自以色列〔艾克

---

60　Luc Reydams, Leuven Working Paper, n. 26 above, p. 22 (internal footnotes omitted). See also the description of State judicial practice in "The Scope and application of the principle of universal jurisdiction: Report of the Secretary-General prepared on the basis of comments and observations of Governments," A/65/181, July 29, 2010, http://daccess-dds-ny.un.org/doc/UNDOC/GEN/N10/467/52/PDF/N1046752. pdf?OpenElement, paras. 55–65; 94–107.

曼（Eichmann）案[61]〕和美国〔德米扬鲁克（Demjanjuk）案[62]〕，承认以色列的普遍管辖权构成引渡的基础，但由于针对的是来自纳粹时代的犯罪嫌疑人，这些控诉具有特殊背景，更有以色列对运用普遍管辖权针对其本国官员的行动进行威胁以及美国主张其他国家对其国民"甚至不应考虑"起诉，[63] 两案的价值被稀释了。

36. 最后，应当指出的是，非洲国家还没有行使过普遍管辖权。[64]

37. 不过，（世界）国际法研究院似乎认为普遍管辖权存在于习惯国际法之中，但发现，如下所述，须以犯罪嫌疑人"现身"为条件。[65] 人们可以发现，（世界）国际法研究院的决议很反常，因为它是在"逮捕令案"判决抑制了人们对普遍管辖权的过分热情，[66]

---

61　*AG of Israel v Eichmann*, 36 ILR 5（District Court of Jerusalem, 1961），and 277（Supreme Court of Israel, 1962）.

62　In re Demjanjuk, 603 F. Supp. 1468（ND Ohio），affirmed, 776 F. 2d 571（6th Cir. 1985），cert. denied, 457 US 1016（1986）.

63　Reydams, Leuven Working Paper, n. 26 above, p. 22.

64　AU-EU Expert Report, n. 5 above, paras. 19, 26, 40.

65　IDI Resolution, n. 3 above.

66　刚果重新提交诉求后，国际法院并没有在"逮捕令案"中对普遍管辖权的合法性问题作出裁定，反而认定不能发现习惯国际法存在于排除在职外交部长所享有的国家管辖豁免和不可侵犯性之例外，即使当外交部长被控犯有战争罪或反人类罪。关于"逮捕令案"的影响，参见 Alain Pellet, "Shaping the Future of International Law: The Role of the World Court in Lawmaking," in Mahnoush H. Arsanjani, et al.（eds.），*Looking to the Future: Essays on International Law in Honor of W. Michael Reisman*（Boston: Brill Nijhoff, 2011），pp. 1065, 1080（"国际法院'逮捕令案'的判决表明法院亦可减慢或足以持续危害现行法律的极其可喜的进化"）；Antonio Cassese, n. 26 above, *J Int'l Criminal Justice* 1, no. 3（2003）: 589-595. 有关豁免权的论述（未在本文讨论），例如，参见 the reports of the ILC Special Rapporteur Roman Anatolevich Kolodkin 以及其他资料，可在如下网页获取："UN Legal Counsel delivers opening remarks to the African Union side-event on the margins of the OEWG on security and use of ICT," http://untreaty. un. org/ilc/guide/4_2. htm。

以及比利时，普遍管辖权的领航员，于 2003 年修改法律将纯粹的普遍管辖权从其法律中剔出[67]从而放弃领航的背景下，反其道而行之，于 2005 年通过的。也就是说，支持纯粹的普遍管辖权（如果真的存在的话）的趋势在逆转。无论如何，（世界）国际法研究院的决议没能阻止目前的逆势，而西班牙则在 2009 年重蹈了比利时 2003 年的覆辙。[68]

38. 对这些案例逐一进行分析会更为理想，那些苦心孤诣的法官和学者们已对此作出努力，不过，他们给出的记录却是相互冲突的评估。仅此即可反映普遍管辖权在国际法中的不确定状态。

39. 对于这一局面，似乎可作几种解释。首先，纯粹的普遍管辖权实际实施的匮乏，可作为表明对这一概念的悦耳支持其实是政治性支持的证据，而不被认为是证明法律确信的证据。

40. 因非盟明文依赖其宣称已将普遍管辖权"蕴含"[69] 其中的《非洲联盟宪法性文件》第 4 条第（h）款，[70] 其在 2009 年的备忘录中对这一概念所表示的支持因此被进一步弱化了。该条确认"在发生战争罪行、灭绝种族和反人类罪的严峻情况下，联盟有权根据首脑会议的决定对某一缔约国进行干预"。该条实际上蕴含一种体制内的集体政治行动机制：其授权联盟，而不是授权个体缔约国，在相关情形下采取行动的权利；被授权的行动是政治性的集体执行行

---

67 See n. 57 above.

68 See n. 58 above.

69 African Union memo, n. 1 above, para. 1.

70 Text accompany n. 49 above.

动，而不是司法执行行动。其并没有提及联盟有权行使普遍管辖权，就更不用说个体缔约国了。在非洲联盟制定这一规定时，这些因素可能还没有获得关注。

41. 有关普遍管辖权的议题被增列进联大会议议程后至今，普遍管辖权的地位并不会因联合国缔约国之间的意见交换而得到加强。此文付梓时（2011 年）已向联大提交声明的缔约国总共只有44 个，约为联合国全体会员国的 25%。[71] 由于宽松模糊的措辞似乎继续处于上风，这些意见交换并未将问题解释得有多清楚。更有可能的是，这一活动似乎还减弱了对这一概念本就微薄的支持。若干国家指出，"普遍管辖权的范围和适用仍是一个在政治和法律上存在巨大争议的问题"。[72] 一些国家，如泰国，则明确反对针对海盗罪和奴隶罪以外的其他罪行行使普遍管辖权。[73] 甚至原本在 2009 年明文支持普遍管辖权"原则"的非盟，似乎在 2010 年也撤回了原有立场。2010 年 10 月提交给第六委员会的非盟声明说：

---

[71] 这些声明可在如下网页获取："Sixth Committee（Legal）—65th session: The scope and application of the principle of universal jurisdiction（Agenda item 86），" http://www.un.org/en/ga/sixth/65/ScopeAppUniJuri.shtml。关于这些声明的概览，参见"The Scope and application of the principle of universal jurisdiction: Report of the Secretary-General prepared on the basis of comments and observations of Governments，" A/65/181, July 29, 2010, http://daccess-dds-ny.un.org/doc/UNDOC/GEN/N10/467/52/PDF/N1046752.pdf?OpenElement。中国于 2010 年提交声明（Statement of China, n. 46 above）。也可参见 Zhu Lijiang, "Chinese Practice in Public International Law: 2009," Chinese Journal of International Law（Chinese Journal of International Law）9, no. 3（2010）: 607, 647, para. 75。

[72] 例如，参见马来西亚的声明，A/C.6/65/SR.12（October 15, 2010），p. 5, para. 26。

[73] 例如，参见泰国的声明，A/C.6/65/SR.11（October 13, 2010），p. 3, para. 12（"除海盗罪外，各国间还没就习惯国际法允许对何种罪行行使普遍管辖权问题普遍达成一致"）；苏丹的声明，A/C.6/65/SR.12（October 15, 2010），p. 4, para. 20；中国的声明，上注 46。

迄今为止，普遍管辖权还没有一个获普遍接受的定义，除海盗罪和奴役罪外其应涵盖何种罪行以及适用条件如何，也还没有取得一致意见。若很少国家提交其普遍管辖权实践信息，那是因为这一原则在大多数国内管辖中几乎还不存在。[74]

另外，不但没有重申《非洲联盟宪法性文件》"蕴含"普遍管辖权原则，该声明现在反而宣称"《非洲联盟宪法性文件》授权联盟在发生战争罪行、灭绝种族和反人类罪的情况下，对其缔约国的事务进行干预"。[75]

42. 其次，少得可怜的实际实施记录即为不存在支持针对海盗罪以外的罪行行使纯粹的普遍管辖权的实在国际习惯法规则之证据。[76] 事实上，甚至没有足够的证据证明存在一项允许行使"普遍关注加现身型普遍管辖权"的国际习惯法规则。

43. 最后，另一解释，由希金斯等法官在"逮捕令案"联合个别意见中提出，即这只是表明各国还没有将该管辖权立法至国际法所允许的最大限度，以及：

虽然这些法官所援引的国家案例法无一恰好立足于严

---

74　A/C. 6/65/SR. 10, October 13, 2010, " Sixth Committee: Summary Record of the 10th Meeting Held at Headquarters, New York, on Wednesday, October 13, 2010, at 10 a. m. , " November 3, 2010, para. 60, http://daccess-ods. un. org/access. nsf/Get?Open&DS = A/C. 6/65/SR. 10 &Lang = E.

75　Ibid. , para. 61.

76　See Statement of China, n. 46 above, Observations, paras. 4-5.

格意义上的普遍管辖权的行使，但该案例法同样不能证明
存在认定此种管辖权为非法的法律确信。简言之，国家立
法和案例法——也就是国家实践——对于普遍管辖权的行
使，态度是中立的。[77]

# 三、"荷花号案"论调（the *Lotus* dictum）的潜在适用

44. 如此定论，希金斯等法官在"逮捕令案"中所附的联合个
别意见实质上主张，在支持国家自由的"荷花号案"论调的适用
中，关键不在于真正的或纯粹的普遍管辖权的行使是否得到实在国
际法的支持，而在于该行使是否为禁止性规范所排除。因没有发现
存在这样的禁止性规范，这些法官得出结论说一国可以行使纯粹的
普遍管辖权（或者被告缺席的普遍管辖权）。[78]

45. 对比之下，纪尧姆院长则直接挑战那一论调，至少是它在
刑事管辖领域的适用。"逮捕令案"中，纪尧姆院长在其个别意见

---

77　Joint Separate Opinion, n. 17 above, para. 45. 英国的解释可参见 Rosalyn Higgins, *Problems and Process: International Law and How We Use It* ( Oxford: Oxford University Press, 1994), pp. 59–61。

78　Joint Separate Opinion, n. 17 above, paras. 49–54, etc.

第14、第15段[79]说：

　　原14. 这一论调几乎不具说服力。其实，国际常设法院自身已确立比利时所援引的那一基本原则，接着却自问"前述因素是否真正适用于刑事管辖权"。它认为，情况可能如此，不然则是，"这一领域法律的全盘的地域性质所确立的一个原则——除非另有明文规定，法律本质上禁止一国将其法院的刑事管辖权扩至其境外"。在这一特定案件中，国际常设法院认为其无须对争议焦点作出裁定。在法国船舶与土耳其船舶发生碰撞的情况下，国际常设法院专门强调所涉犯罪行为的后果可被当作发生在土耳其领土上，因此土耳其的刑事控诉"可从有关这一所谓地域原则的观点中找到正当理由"。

　　原15. 在1927年当时条约法极其罕有的情况下，国际常设法院不对争议焦点作裁定是可以理解的。不过今天情况不同了，对我来说——则完全不同了。宣扬国家主权平等的《联合国宪章》被通过，新兴国家登上历史舞台，非殖民化运动的诞生，强化了地域原则。国际刑法本身已经

---

79　President Guillaume, "Separate Opinion in Arrest Warrant," *ICJ Reports 2002*, pp. 35, 43. 对"荷花号案"论调的进一步批判，参见 Judge Simma, "Declaration, in Accordance with International Law of the Unilateral Declaration of Independence in Respect of Kosovo ( Request for Advisory Opinion)," *ICJ Reports 2010*, http://www.icj-cij.org/docket/files/141/15993.pdf; Sienho Yee, "Notes on the International Court of Justice ( Part 4): The Kosovo Advisory Opinion," *Chinese Journal of International Law* 9, no. 4 (2010): 763, paras. 22-26。

经历了非常大的发展且形成了一个令人印象深刻的法律体系。在很多情形下，它都确认犯罪行为地以外的国家授权其法院对现身于其领土的犯罪者进行起诉的可能性（或实质上是义务）。但是决不可想象，世界上任何一个国家均应授权其法院对这些犯罪进行起诉，不管作案者和受害者是谁，也不管犯罪者将被发现于何地。再说，如此行事，将令司法陷于完全混乱的境地，还将鼓励强国为其利益而故意打着界限模糊的"国际社会"之代理人的旗号肆意妄为。与某些国际法学家所提倡的相反，这样的发展方向并不代表法律的进步，反倒是一种倒行逆施。

46. 纪尧姆院长的观点很有说服力。"荷花号案"的论调在该案中是没有必要的，其生命力来源于对其不加批判的复述和随从。

47. 从某种程度上说，这一争论似乎关乎哪项隐含规则是否适当。在国际常设法院作出判决时，各国仍然坚持使用武力解决国际争端这一古老权力法则。国家自由被认为至高无上因此应当优先考虑，这大概是自然的事。这就是"荷花号案"论调的适用后面所隐含的规则。不管怎样，自1927年作出判决之日以来，发展态势不再支持这一观点。自从1928年签订于巴黎的《凯洛格—白里安公约》首次表示放弃使用武力作为国家政策的工具以及《联合国宪章》第2条第4款重申这一立场以来，国家自由现被置于领土完整和国家政治独立的从属地位。这是当今整个国际法律体系最重要的隐喻规则。用纪尧姆院长的话说，这些新发展强化了属地原则。"荷花号案"论调因此可被认为已经过时，至少在刑事管辖权方面是如此。这也是（世界）国际法研究院一些成员在其 2005 年有关该专题的决议的审议至通过过程中提出来的观点。[80] 事实上，在某些领域，各国已通过条约的方式积极推翻国际常设法院在"荷花号案"中有关刑事管辖权的裁决。[81]

48. 在这样的背景下，中国也反对"荷花号案"论调。其于 2010 年向联大提交的有关普遍管辖权问题的声明中明文表示：

> 管辖权是国家主权的重要组成部分。根据国家主权平等的原则，一国确立和行使管辖权不应损害其他国家的主权。因此一国管辖权的确立应当以该国与所涉案件之间存在有效和充分的联系因素为前提条件，并应将其限于一个合理的范围。[82]

49. 人们不由得充分期待在这一方面能够得到进一步的发展。在"荷花号案"论调在这一领域被打败之前，可以想象，各国可能会以反对普遍管辖权为由阻止其适用，因为"荷花号案"论调的适用基础，根据"逮捕令案"的联合个别意见，是这样的一个事

---

80　See IDI, 71（Ⅱ）Annuaire, n. 4 above, p. 245（The Rapporteur）；p. 258（Frowein）.

81　E. g., 1952 Brussels Convention for the Unification of Certain Rules Relating to Penal Jurisdiction in Matters of Collision or other Incidents of Navigation, art. 1; UNCLOS, art. 97.

82　中国的声明，上注 46，联合国英译本，有关评论见第 1 段。该译本将"管辖权"译为"sovereignty"。本文原文使用"Jurisdiction"代替"sovereignty"。

实——不存在可表明普遍管辖权为非法的法律确信的证据。一国仅是无声地不支持普遍管辖权未必能够阻止其国民被适用普遍管辖权，因为适用"荷花号案"论调的后果是，它可能允许国际法虽未授权但也未禁止其管辖的国家行使管辖权。这意味着，就"荷花号案"论调的适用而言，作出明确的反对会有所裨益，"外交风味"的模糊或者沉默可能存在风险。

## 四、实施普遍管辖权（如允许）的潜在限制

50. 通过以上分析，我们可以发现，普遍管辖权可能是维护国际社会基本价值、促进和保护人员，以及对抗有罪不罚的积极工具。其消极方面则是普遍管辖权的行使与主权和主权平等原则相冲突，且容易遭政治滥用，包括出现在选择性诉讼中的差别待遇，从而破坏国际关系的稳定。[83] 如果我们假定法律允许出于某些原因运用这一原理或原则，并试图在减少这一工具的副作用的同时收获其果实，我们可以设想将普遍管辖权的行使置于一系列条件之下，或者这些条件是否应当构成普遍管辖权"定义"的一部分，例如：（1）将普遍管辖权的行使限于最严重的罪行，例如，除海盗罪外，还包括奴役罪、灭绝种族罪、反人类罪和严重的战争罪行；（2）领土所属国具有优先权；（3）适用"清白原则"；[84]（4）要求有最高

---

[83]　See Henry Kissinger, n. 19 above.

[84]　See Sienho Yee, "The Tu Quoque Argument as a Defence to International Crimes, Prosecution, or Punishment," *Chinese Journal of International Law* 3, no. 1（2004）：87–133.

国家当局启动行使的决定；（5）尊重可适用于官员和国家的豁免权；（6）能够获得某一国际甄别机制的认可；（7）犯罪嫌疑人现身。笔者对此不一一作讨论，只对现身要求或条件作些评论。

51. 似乎这一观点获得广泛的支持——不存在一项允许在缺乏现身条件的情况下行使普遍管辖权的习惯国际法规则。[85] 在缺乏条约支持的情况下，犯罪嫌疑人现身可使"普遍管辖权"的行使合法化的观点并无充分的理据支持。再者，基于某种理由被允许行使普遍管辖权时，现身条件在哪一时间点被触发，并还取得一致意见。似乎对大概仍依赖于"荷花号案"论调的"逮捕令案"法官希金斯等人来说，关于现身角色的这一认定本身并没有显示犯罪嫌疑人的现身因此成为行使普遍管辖权的条件；对于试图行使普遍管辖权的国家，只需要没有针对它的禁止性规范即可。这样的现身条件在种种关于引渡或起诉的条约条款中的存在——在他们看来，"清楚地，这预想在有关领土上现身"——没有理由得出相反的结论，因此现身是必要的。[86] 对这些法官来说，"如果认为某人在审判当时人身须被置于管辖，那将是一个保证公平审判的审慎的保证，但与国际法认可的管辖根据没有多大关系"。[87] 必须指出的是，这一观点，将现身条件贬低至仅是保证公平审判的一个审慎的程序性要求，后果具有深远的影响，且与规避缺席审判的国际刑法的趋向大相径庭。实

---

85　参见以色列的声明，A/C. 6/65/SR. 12（October 15, 2010），p. 3, para. 9（"很多国家同意被告应当在法院地国现身"）。

86　Joint Separate Opinion, n. 17 above, in particular, para. 57（emphasis in the original）.

87　Ibid. , para. 56.

际上，这一趋向能够反映对我们安身立命的世界所持的一种态度或观点，而不仅只是一种对更为公正的审判的追求。将现身条件视为程序性要求之观点的深远影响将会更加持久——或呈倍数增长——当其与"逮捕令案"的联合个别意见极力赞成的"荷花号案"论调的适用扭在一起捆绑使用的时候（因两者皆偏向起诉国的自由权）。[88]

52. 根据（世界）国际法研究院以及其他人士的观点，该触发点出现得更早一些。（世界）国际法研究院决议第 3 段（b）称：

> 除调查行动和引渡请求外，行使普遍管辖权也要求被控犯罪嫌疑人现身于起诉国领土或悬挂该国国旗的船舶或依其法律注册的航空器上，或者犯罪嫌疑人为其他合法形式所控制。

根据报告人，该段：

> 反对绝对普遍管辖权的理论，坚持犯罪嫌疑人现身于起诉国领土这一条件。不过，与逮捕令的签发不同，它的确允许任何一国开展对个体不造成实质损害的调查活动。同样地，各国应享有请求引渡的自由，尽管被请求国并无义务满足这样的要求。[89]

---

88　这存在导致出现起诉国自由最大化——某一类型的"荷花号案最高自由"的危险，参见 Sienho Yee, n. 79 above, *Chinese Journal of International Law* (2010): 763, para. 26。

89　IDI Annuaire, n. 4 above, p. 208 (the Rapporteur introducing the draft resolution).

这一路径具有一定的合理性，但仍然存在三个主要问题。第一，如果犯罪嫌疑人在被请求国拥有一个官方职位，那么被请求国需要作出一个艰难的决定，否则不大可能会满足请求国的引渡要求。如果被请求国非犯罪嫌疑人国籍国（犯罪嫌疑人或官员在外旅行），那么考虑可能会有所不同，引渡请求完全有可能获得满足。

53. 第二，现行司法协助制度或者引渡条约实际上可能实行强制性引渡，因为这些条约中至少有部分规定，如果请求国能证实管辖权和案件证据已表面成立以及普遍管辖权可被认为已足以满足行使管辖权的条件，被请求国则有义务移送犯罪嫌疑人。如何解释（世界）国际法研究院报告人的观点——被请求国无义务（源自普遍管辖权法本身）满足这样的请求，以及被请求国需要遵守的其他类型法律规定的义务，成为一个十分重要的问题。换言之，在主张普遍管辖权的场合下，依其他类型法律负有满足请求之一般义务，该一般义务是否应当存在例外？

54. 第三，在某些国家，除逮捕和引渡外，调查的启动可能会引发一系列强制性司法程序。这一低层次的强制性司法程序依然会带来严重问题。主张为针对犯罪嫌疑人现身的调查之启动设定条件，可能是过分的要求，很多国家将极可能予以拒绝。或者一个折中方案可为，犯罪嫌疑人在起诉国现身可被设定为强制司法程序发动的条件。

55. 这一讨论应给每个行事谨慎的国家发出警告，即普遍管辖权的潜在实施与所有司法和警务合作条约之间的关系，以及现身条件与这一关系的牵连，是一个呼唤紧急考察的议题。它或希望通过修改这些条约，以确保一个宽松的现身条件不会为其国际关系活动带来问题。

# 五、结语

56. 真正或纯粹的普遍管辖权是一种仅以所涉罪行的受普遍关注性质为根据的管辖权。普遍管辖权的概念和逻辑合乎情理，因为每个国家均对受普遍关注之事拥有权益。普遍管辖权可成为国际体系维护其权益，保护人权和对抗有罪不罚的强有力工具。然而，一国行使普遍管辖权可能会侵犯另一国的国家主权和主权平等，亦有可能滥用，从而破坏国际关系的稳定。

57. 这些正反两面以及其他方面的因素对国际法的形成过程产生了这样或那样的影响，以致迄今为止只有针对海盗罪的普遍管辖权已为国际法所接受。针对其他罪行的"纯粹的普遍关注型管辖权"目前还不存在。"普遍关注加现身型管辖权"的国家实践证据尚不足以充分证明一项习惯国际法规则已因此形成。允许"普遍关注加条约、现身并体制内属地或属人型管辖权"，或者"普遍关注加条约、现身型管辖权"的条约实践只局限于特定的条约体制。鉴于这种局面，"荷花号案"论调及现身条件的潜在适用——尤其是关于其要求轻微、程序性观点，可能具有重要意义而值得关注。

58. 在 2002 年，当希金斯等法官的联合个别意见发现普遍管辖权的某种演化趋向之时，[90] 国际法院却在"逮捕令案"中对普遍管辖权合法性问题保持引人注目的沉默，自那以来，追求"纯粹的普遍管辖权"的进程一直呈"下降趋势"。此后的下降趋势很大程度上可能源于对该案的审慎判决。该判决可被认为以一种巧妙的方式，帮助将某些冷静元素注入国际关系当中。[91] 随着比利时和西班牙现已通过收窄其法律适用范围从而放弃纯粹的普遍管辖权，追求纯粹的普遍管辖权的进程似乎成了一列正在行驶的没了机车头的列车。

# 六、后记

59. 本文于 2011 年首次发表。自 2009 年以来，联合国大会关于普遍管辖权的辩论表明，人们对普遍管辖权的概念、范围和适用的认知很混乱，这是促使笔者发表本文的动机。本文试图提出一个笔者自认为是对普遍管辖权的恰当理解，并指出针对某一罪行的普遍管辖权是否存在，取决于正常的造法过程或法律形成过程，而非取决于任何实体规范的先验逻辑延伸。这就需要对这方面的国家实践作更加严格的考量。

60. 自本文首次发表以来，关于这些问题的后续发展似乎使笔

---

90  Joint Separate Opinion, n. 17 above, paras. 45-52.

91  关于"逮捕令案"影响的更充分的评估，参见 Alain Pellet, n. 66 above。

者的观点，还有笔者的观察——纯粹普遍管辖权呈"下降趋势"，得到了进一步的支持。国际法院 2012 年 2 月 3 日关于"德国诉意大利案"（*Germany v Italy*）的判决[92]认定（虽然不是很明确，但实质如此）普遍管辖权并非以主行为的性质为根据，而是取决于正常的造法或法律形成过程。联大的辩论尚未消除混乱；事实上，在 2018 年 12 月 20 日通过的一项决议中，联大仍称其"认识到各国所表达的意见各式各样，包括对滥用或误用普遍管辖权的关切，并承认若要取得进展，需在第六委员会继续讨论普遍管辖权的范围和适用问题"[93]此外，学术界也对笔者所表达的观点持开放态度。2012 年，本文被翻译成俄文发表于《俄罗斯法学论刊》[94]接着，一个重要的组织邀请笔者和这一领域的少数专家召开闭门咨询会，可以看出笔者论点的影响受到了关注。2013 年 4 月，笔者应美国国际法学会邀请，将本文以"需对普遍管辖权作更加严格的评估"为题在该学会年会上作报告。[95]

---

[92] Jurisdictional Immunities of the State (*Germany v Italy: Greece intervening*), Judgment, *ICJ Reports 2012*, p. 99.

[93] A/RES/73/208, December 20, 2018 ("*Noting* the constructive dialogue in the Sixth Committee, including in the context of its working group, recognizing the diversity of views expressed by States, including concerns expressed in relation to the abuse or misuse of the principle of universal jurisdiction, and acknowledging, in order to make progress, the need for continuing discussions on the scope and application of the principle of universal jurisdiction in the Sixth Committee").

[94] Сиенхо Йии (Вухан, Китай) Универсальная юрисдикция: понятие, теория и практика, РОССИЙСКИЙ ЮРИДИЧЕСКИЙ ЖУРНАЛ (*Russian Juridical Journal*) 85, no. 4 (2012): 7-31.

[95] Sienho Yee, "A Call for a More Rigorous Assessment of Universal Jurisdiction," *ASIL Proceedings* 107 (2013): 242.

61. 就"下降趋势"而言，西班牙已通过立法加以延续。[96] 这一趋势如此，以致一位评论人士在捍卫普遍管辖权时把他的文章题目定为"普遍管辖权并非在消失：从'全球强制者'型普遍管辖权（'globe enforcer' universal jurisdiction）到'不提供安全港'型普遍管辖权（'no safe haven' universal jurisdiction）的转换"。[97] 他说：按"全球强制者"型普遍管辖权概念，各国可行使普遍管辖权，因为其扮演着这样的角色——预防在世界任何地方发生国际核心罪行并惩罚在世界任何地方所犯的国际核心罪行；按"不提供安全港"型普遍管辖权概念，各国可行使普遍管辖权以避免国际核心罪行参与者有藏身之处。[98] 如此看来，他似乎中意"普遍关注加现身型管辖权"，即如笔者在本文第 8 段第（2）小段以及本文其他地方所述。但如同笔者所指出的那样，这一类型的管辖权并非真正的普遍管辖权；法院地国这一联系因素即足以构成管辖的基础。即使如此，如上所述，尚无足够的国家实践支持其成为一项习惯国际法。

62. 有意思的是，在其 2012 年 7 月 20 日关于"与起诉或引渡义务有关的问题案（比利时诉塞内加尔）"［*Questions relating to the Obligation to Prosecute or Extradite（Belgium v Senegal）*］的判决[99]中，

---

96　See Ashifa Kassam, "Spain Regressing on Human Rights, Says Judge Who Pursued Pinochet," *The Guardian*, February 14, 2014, http://www.theguardian.com/world/2014/feb/14/spain-human-rights-judge-baltasar-garzon. 只有阿根廷近年来好像在没有明确的国内法基础的情况下展现了一些尚难以评估的激进趋势。见本书第 58—61、130—134 页。

97　Maximo Langer, "Universal Jurisdiction is Not Disappearing: The Shift from 'Global Enforcer' to 'No Safe Haven' Universal Jurisdiction," *Journal of International Criminal Justice* 13（2015）: 245-256.

98　Ibid., p. 249.

99　*ICJ Reports 2012*, p. 422.

国际法院看似并不满意《禁止酷刑公约》本身的效力——案子只涉及公约，且公约本身足以解决案子所涉问题——觉得还需要借助普遍管辖权概念的力量。它这样做了，但未对其含义作出任何解释，也没有就针对所涉罪行的普遍管辖权的存在给出任何支持性分析。在判决的第74、第75、第84、第91、第118段，国际法院只是亮出"普遍管辖权"一词，而不顾如下事实："逮捕令案"联合个别意见是把《禁止酷刑公约》作为不构成普遍管辖权的例证来使用的，且批评把公约第5条称作"普遍管辖权"是对"该用语的不严谨的使用"。[100] 结果，我们不知道，在该案中，国际法院心目中的普遍管辖权概念究竟是哪一种版本。于是，国际法院以这样的一种方式使用该术语，考虑到这一使用属附带性论调（*obiter dicta*），这可能是在给人们带来混乱和误导——当然没有必要如此。

63. 不管怎样，世人所能期望相关决策者的，是他们严格遵循这方面的造法或法律形成运作机制，而所有审慎决策者能够而且应当做的，是审慎、严格地运用这样的运作机制。其余则取决于作为国际社会主要造法者的各国。[101]

---

100　Joint Separate Opinion, n. 17 above, para. 41.

101　本后记（第59—63段）最先发表在 Alexander Orakhelashvili（ed.），*Research Handbook on Jurisdiction and Immunities in International Law*（Cheltenham: Edward Elgar Publishing 2015），pp. 106-109。本处稍作修改。

# 普遍管辖权的国家实践研究

王佳　易显河

普遍管辖权一般指的是国家刑事管辖权中的一种，目前并没有条约等国际规范对其加以界定。[1] 在实践中，国际社会对于普遍管辖权的概念、范围和适用等问题的认识存在明显分歧，在一些案件中引发了极大争议，甚至可能影响国际法律秩序和国际关系的健康发展。鉴于迄今为止围绕普遍管辖权未形成有约束力的国际法律文件，对普遍管辖权的国家实践进行分析格外重要，一方面在国际法形成过程中，可以通过相关研究试图影响国际法朝着对中国有利的方向发展；另一方面可以根据他国行使普遍管辖权的可能，对中国官员的外访问题进行提前研判。

本研究对普遍管辖权概念与分类的阐述和分析采用易显河于

---

[1]　虽然一般是在刑事管辖的背景下援引普遍管辖，但是普遍管辖权可能存在民事维度。实践中围绕民事普遍管辖权的问题存有争议。本文主要分析刑事层面的普遍管辖。有关民事普遍管辖权问题，可参见 The American Law Institute, *Restatement of the Law Fourth, The Foreign Relations Law of the United States, Selected Topics in Treaties, Jurisdiction, and Sovereign Immunity* ( St. Paul: American Law Institute Publishers, 2018), pp. 211, 215。

2011 年在《普遍管辖权：概念、逻辑和现状》（Universal Jurisdiction: Concept, Logic, and Reality）[2] 一文中提出的框架和分析、分类，进而对于不同地域范围的国家的普遍管辖权实践进行了梳理和分析。本文选取研究对象国家的主要依据为二：其一，其实践具有一定代表性；其二，相关资料可得。本文所研究的国家实践主要包括条约实践、国内立法、司法实践等，资料来源是《涉普遍关注型管辖权的主要国家实践情况选编》。在研究思路方面，本文的第一部分首先对普遍管辖权进行界定与分类；第二部分在分类的基础上，对主要国家的普遍管辖权实践进行总结；第三部分为结论，一方面对普遍管辖权的国家实践发展情况与趋势进行研判，另一方面对中国的相关实践提出建议。

# 一、普遍管辖权的概念与分类

国际社会围绕普遍管辖权的概念存在明显分歧，在实践中，普遍管辖权常在不同场合被赋予不同含义，可以根据"普遍性"的强度不同，对人们所说的普遍管辖权进行分类。

## （一）普遍管辖权的概念

目前，国际社会围绕普遍管辖权的概念存在明显分歧，几乎不

---

2 Sienho Yee, "Universal Jurisdiction: Concept, Logic, and Reality," *Chinese Journal of International Law*, no. 10 (2011): 503-530, https://doi.org/10.1093/chinesejil/jmr041；中文版参见易显河《普遍管辖权的概念、逻辑和现状》，易显书译，《国际法学刊》2019 年第 1 期，第 107 页。

可能对普遍管辖权作出具有共识的界定。[3] 不过，很多定义和评论似乎将普遍管辖权定义为一种在控罪与企图行使管辖权的国家法律系统之间"缺乏"（absence）正常的管辖联系因素的管辖权。[4] 正如国际法研究院（*Institut de droit international*）在其 2005 年有关普遍管辖权的决议中所称：刑事方面的普遍管辖权作为一种补充性的管辖依据，指的是一国具有起诉和惩罚（如被定罪）犯罪嫌疑人的权能，不问被控罪行犯于何地，亦不问是否存在国际法承认的加害人国籍或被害人国籍，抑或其他管辖依据等任何联系因素。[5]

不过，控罪与企图行使管辖权的国家之间缺乏正常的管辖联系因素只能说是普遍管辖权的表面特征，而非其本质。因为，国家可在不具有正常的管辖联系因素下行使管辖权，则必定说明其背后有特殊的依据存在，否则便意味着国家可随意行使管辖权。事实上，普遍管辖权的背后依据是其所针对的罪行是为国际社会所"普遍关注"（universal concern）的罪行。国家为惩治特定罪行，即使国家与犯罪嫌疑人、受害者，或犯罪发生地没有具体的联系，也能够基

---

3　当然，比较特殊的是，国际社会对于发生在公海上的海盗行为作为普遍管辖的对象没有争议，本文不专门讨论海盗罪。

4　易显河：《普遍管辖权的概念、逻辑和现状》，易显书译，《国际法学刊》2019 年第 1 期，第 107 页。

5　Institute of International Law, "Universal criminal jurisdiction with regard to the crime of genocide (2005)," "crimes against humanity and war crimes," para. 1, accessed June 8, 2023, https://www.idi-iil. org/app/uploads/2017/06/2005_kra_03_en. pdf.

于国际社会的"普遍关注"而行使普遍管辖权。[6] 因此，可以将此种类型的管辖权称为"普遍关注型管辖权"，以便与"属地管辖权""属人管辖权""保护管辖权"形成对照，因上述三种管辖权之命名主要基于管辖权背后的依据，或为领土、或为国籍、或为国家利益保护。

## （二）普遍管辖权的分类

在实践中，普遍管辖权常在不同场合被赋予不同含义，可以根据"普遍性"的强度不同，对人们所说的普遍管辖权进行分类。[7]

第一，"纯粹的普遍关注型管辖权"（pure universal concern jurisdiction）。此种类型的管辖权仅以罪行受普遍关注为依据，也可称为"纯粹的普遍管辖权"（pure universal jurisdiction）或"真正的普遍管辖权"（true universal jurisdiction）。有人也称之为"缺席的普遍管辖权"（universal jurisdiction in absentia）。[8] 该类型管辖权包含以下两种情形：其一，一国单方主张纯粹的普遍管辖权；其二，假设存在一项条约，允许缔约国对非缔约国国民在缔约国以外的第三国领土上所犯的罪行主张纯粹的普遍管辖权。[9]

---

6  The American Law Institute, *Restatement of the Law Fourth, The Foreign Relations Law of the United States, Selected Topics in Treaties, Jurisdiction, and Sovereign Immunity* ( St. Paul: American Law Institute Publishers, 2018), p. 210.

7  对于普遍管辖权的分类，本文参见易显河《普遍管辖权的概念、逻辑和现状》，易显书译，《国际法学刊》2019 年第 1 期，第 110—111 页。

8  由于该术语可能会和"缺席审判"（trial in absentia）相混淆，本文未予采用。

9  第二种情形下，在涉及第三国问题上，事实上条约并不比其缔约国拥有更大的权限。

第二，"普遍关注加现身型管辖权"（universal concern plus presence jurisdiction）。此种类型的管辖权的依据除罪行受普遍关注外，还有犯罪人现身于该国。这并非严格意义上的普遍管辖权，因为犯罪嫌疑人的现身可能会使此种管辖权被认定为"属地管辖权"，而当现身持续至其归化取得国籍时，还很可能被认定为"属人管辖权"。而如果只是短暂现身的话，则有人称为普遍管辖权，另有人则称为带有联系因素的管辖权。

第三，"普遍关注加条约、现身型管辖权"（universal concern plus treaty and presence jurisdiction）。此种类型的管辖权的依据相较于第二种增加了条约规定的义务或权利。这种管辖权的行使除基于普遍关注和现身外，还要求存在条约，即条约允许其缔约国针对现身于起诉国的第三国国民就其在第三国所犯的受普遍关注的罪行行使管辖权。

第四，"普遍关注加条约、现身并体制内属地或属人型管辖权"（universal concern plus treaty, presence and intra-regime territoriality or nationality jurisdiction）。此种类型的管辖权除须满足第三种的依据外，还增加了如下条件：犯罪嫌疑人或罪行必须与创设条约体制的某一条约缔约国之间存在领土、国籍或被害人国籍等联系因素。体制内属人联系因素可表述为：条约允许缔约国 A 对现身于其领土的缔约国 C 之国民 B，就其被控犯于非缔约国 D 的受普遍关注罪行进行起诉。体制内属地联系因素可表述为：条约允许缔约国 A 对现身于其领土的第三国（非条约缔约国）国民 B，就其被控犯于缔约国 C 领土上的受普遍关注罪行进行起诉。

这四种类型中，除了第一种外，其他的各种都不是真正的普遍管辖权。因为第二种情形至第四种情形都要求现身，其中后两种还要求现身引发的条约义务。其中，第二种情形虽然已经偏离了纯粹的普遍关注型管辖权的轨道，但比其他情形更接近纯粹的普遍关注型管辖权。第三、第四种情形更加不属于真正意义上的普遍管辖权，实际上是基于条约的管辖权行使。本文将以上述四种类型作为分析框架，对于国家实践情况进行分类评析。

## 二、普遍管辖权的国家实践归类与分析

本文对分布在欧洲、亚洲、美洲、非洲、大洋洲的 31 个具有代表性的国家的普遍管辖权实践进行了分析，具体分析内容参见"涉普遍关注型管辖权的主要国家实践情况选编"。本文只选取若干主要国家为代表，简要地对其有关普遍管辖权的国家实践进行归类与分析。值得说明的是，虽然本文将某一国家的实践列为 4 种类型之一，但并不意味着该国只行使一种类型的所谓普遍管辖权，本文只是侧重于国家主要的、具有特色的实践。

### （一）纯粹的普遍关注型管辖权

从 20 世纪末到 21 世纪初，以比利时、西班牙为代表的国家行使纯粹的普遍关注型管辖权的实践颇为令人瞩目，但是目前上述国家的此种实践已经式微。不过，阿根廷近年来在行使纯粹的普遍关

注型管辖权方面比较积极，这或许证明了这一类型管辖权的发展存
在反复、波折和不确定。

## 1. 比利时

2003 年前，比利时对某些罪行行使纯粹的普遍关注型管辖权，
且被认为"拥有着世界上范围最广泛的普遍管辖权法律"。[10] 1993 年
6 月，比利时通过《关于惩罚严重违反 1949 年 8 月 12 日日内瓦公
约及 1977 年 6 月 8 日附加议定书罪行的法案》。根据该法案，任何
犯有战争罪的犯罪嫌疑人都可以在比利时被起诉，不论其国籍、被
害人国籍、犯罪时间和犯罪地点，也不论该人是否现身比利时境
内。[11] 该法体现了缺席的普遍管辖原则，且根据该法成立了专门负
责调查国际罪行的机构。[12] 1999 年 2 月，该法得到修订，将普遍管
辖的罪行扩大到灭绝种族罪和反人类罪，同时规定犯罪嫌疑人不能
主张任何种类的豁免，并重新命名为《关于惩罚严重违反国际人道
法罪行的法案》。[13] 由此，比利时在立法方面建立起当时最为激进的
纯粹的普遍关注型管辖权。

在司法实践方面，比利时法院受理了大量的案件。被告包括伊

---

10　Malvina Halberstam, "Belgium's Universal Jurisdiction Law: Vindication of International Justice or
Pursuit of Politics?"*Cardozo Law Review* 25, no. 1 (2003), p. 247.

11　Stijin Deklerck（涂建平）：《普遍性管辖原则：比利时的〈反暴行法〉》，朱利江译，
《北大国际法与比较法评论》2004 年第 3 卷第 1 辑，第 296 页。

12　Wolfgang Kaleck, "From Pinochet to Rumsfeld: Universal Jurisdiction in Europe 1998－2008,"
*Michigan Journal of International Law* 30, no. 3 (2009), p. 932.

13　Stijin Deklerck（涂建平）：《普遍性管辖原则：比利时的〈反暴行法〉》，朱利江译，
《北大国际法与比较法评论》2004 年第 3 卷第 1 辑，第 296—297 页。

拉克总统萨达姆、古巴国务委员会主席卡斯特罗、巴勒斯坦领袖阿拉法特、乍得总统哈布雷、智利前总统皮诺切特、以色列总理沙龙、刚果外交部长耶罗迪亚等政要。在一些案件中，比利时法院对被告作出了有罪判决。比如，2001 年 4 月，在第一起依据普遍管辖权提起的"四名布塔雷人案"（Butare Four case, 2001）中，四名被告被判灭绝种族罪，分别被判处 12 年至 20 年有期徒刑。[14]

不过，纯粹的普遍关注型管辖权的热潮在比利时的持续时间并不长。两方面的原因使比利时的纯粹的普遍关注型管辖权实践宣告失败。第一，2002 年 2 月，国际法院就刚果诉比利时逮捕令案作出判决，认定比利时于 2000 年签发针对刚果外交部长耶罗迪亚的逮捕令侵犯其外交豁免。[15] 虽然国际法院没有处理刚果提出的"行使缺席的普遍管辖权违反国际法"问题，但比利时国会为使立法与国际法院判决保持一致，于 2003 年 4 月修订了《关于惩罚严重违反国际人道法罪行的法案》，修订后的法案大大限制了适用普遍管辖的条件。[16] 第二，2003 年 3 月，受害人向比利时法院起诉，指控美国时任总统布什、副总统切尼、国务卿鲍威尔等在 1991 年海湾战争期间

---

14  Luc Reydams, "Belgium's First Application of Universal Jurisdiction: The Butare Four Case," *Journal of International Criminal Justice*, no. 1（2003）:433–434.

15  参见 Arrest Warrant of 11 April 2000（*Democratic Republic of the Congo v Belgium*）, Judgment, *I. C. J. Reports 2002*。

16  修订后的法律规定，只有在被告人和比利时存在以下联系时，受害人才可以提起诉讼:（1）被告人位于比利时境内;（2）犯罪发生在比利时境内;（3）受害人为比利时公民或已经在比利时连续居住满三年，否则只能由比利时国家检察机关提起公诉。同时规定，只有在国际法允许的情况下，才可以不考虑豁免事宜。参见 Roozbeh（Rudy）B. Baker, "Universal Jurisdiction and The Case of Belgium: A Critical Assessment," *ILSA Journal of Int'l & Comparative Law* 16, no. 1（2009）: 149–163。

犯下战争罪行。在美国强烈的政治压力下，比利时政府于 2003 年 8 月 5 日宣布废除普遍管辖权立法，将有关国际罪行和普遍管辖权的法律纳入新《刑法典》中。至此，比利时有关普遍管辖权的专门立法，连同曾经的先锋立场和激进实践，彻底落幕。

根据比利时新《刑法典》第 136 条的规定和 2010 年比利时向联大第六委员会提交的材料，国际罪行主要包括灭绝种族罪、反人类罪、战争罪、恐怖主义犯罪、贩运人口罪、切割女性生殖器罪等。此外，只有在被控犯有国际罪行的被告人是比利时公民或居民，或犯罪被害人是比利时人或在罪行发生时在比利时已经连续居住达三年，或条约要求比利时进行管辖的前提下，比利时法院才有权行使管辖权。[17] 因此，目前比利时有关普遍管辖权的国家实践基本属于"普遍关注加条约、现身"型。在大大限制了普遍管辖权条件后，比利时有关普遍管辖权立法已与欧洲大多数国家别无二致，甚至比有些国家法律的限制还要更多。[18]

## 2. 西班牙

在 20 世纪末至 21 世纪初期，西班牙被公认为采取了"绝对的普遍管辖权"（absolute universal jurisdiction）。[19] 根据其立法和司法

---

17　Universal Jurisdiction in Europe—The State of the Art, Human Rights Watch, June 2006, accessed May 8, 2024, https://www.refworld.org/reference/themreport/hrw/2006/en/63206.

18　Arrêt de la Cour de cassation de Belgique dans l'affaire Sharon & Yaron, Belgium, accessed June 8, 2023, https://www.derechos.org/intlaw/doc/belsharon.html.

19　"Spain: Practice to Rule 157: Jurisdiction over War Crimes," IRCR, IHL Database, Customary IHL, accessed June 8, 2023, https://ihl-databases.icrc.org/en/customary-ihl/v2/rule157?country=es.

实践，这一时期西班牙的相关实践可称为纯粹的普遍关注型管辖权。

西班牙最早有关普遍管辖权的立法见于 1985 年《司法权力组织法》第 23 条第 4 款，根据该款，"西班牙法院对于西班牙公民或者外国人在西班牙领域外实施的以下任一犯罪，同样享有管辖权：（1）灭绝种族罪；（2）恐怖主义犯罪；（3）海盗罪和非法劫持航空器罪；（4）伪造外国货币罪；（5）卖淫罪；（6）非法贩运精神药物、毒品和麻醉品罪；（7）根据国际公约或者条约应当在西班牙追诉的其他犯罪"。[20] 从字面含义看，第 23 条第 4 款对于普遍管辖权的适用没有规定任何限制条件，是"世界上最自由的普遍管辖权法令"。[21]

这一时期的司法实践也体现了西班牙法院对纯粹的普遍关注型管辖权的坚持。比如，在 1998 年的希林格和卡瓦洛案（Scilingo and Cavallo case, 1998）中，西班牙高等法院指出："某些具有强行法和普遍性质的行为被认为是违反国际法的罪行。实施这些行为的最先后果就是由全人类共同确认其犯罪性质，即使犯罪人国籍国或者犯罪发生地国的国内法不加禁止……相反，全人类及所有国

---

20　"The Scope and Application of the Principle of Universal Jurisdiction: Information Provided by Spain," United Nations General Assembly 66th session, Spain, June 20, 2011, accessed June 8, 2023, https://www.un.org/en/ga/sixth/66/ScopeAppUniJuri_StatesComments/Spain%20（S%20to%20E）.pdf.

21　Fausto Pocar and Magali Maystre, "The Principle of Complementarity: A Means towards a More Pragmatic Enforcement of the Goal Pursued by Universal Jurisdiction?" in Morten Bergsmo（ed.）, *Complementarity and the Exercise of Universal Jurisdiction of Core International Crimes* [Brussels: Torkel Opsahl Academic EPublisher（TOAEP）, 2010], p. 166.

家在起诉和惩治这些罪行上有着同等的利益。为确保有效满足这种利益，国际法赋予所有国家起诉这些罪行的管辖权（即普遍管辖权）。"[22]

在 21 世纪初至 2009 年，西班牙经历了纯粹的普遍关注型管辖权向普遍关注加条约、现身型管辖权的过渡。这一时期西班牙的国家实践体现出以下特点：第一，司法先行于立法。虽然《司法权力组织法》第 23 条第 4 款没有大幅修订，但法院在解释和适用时已经呈现"相对化"的趋势，将"与西班牙相关联"（relevant link with Spain）作为限制条件。第二，过渡并非一帆风顺，普遍管辖权的适用在上下级法院间较为割裂，由绝对到有限的进程反复周折。

2009 年后，西班牙完全放弃了纯粹的普遍关注型管辖权的理念，开始对普遍管辖权适用条件进行限制。随着 2009 年和 2014 年对《司法权力组织法》的两次修订，西班牙对普遍管辖权的国家实

---

22　"Texto completo de la Sentencia 16/2005," Audiencia Nacional Sala De Lo Penal Seccion Tercera, Spain, April 19, 2005, accessed June 8, 2023, http://www.derechos.org/nizkor/espana/juicioral/doc/sentencia.html#5.%20SOBRE%20LA%20APLICABILIDAD.

践最终体现为普遍关注加条约、现身型管辖权。[23] 即一方面主张
"依据国际法和国际条约行使普遍管辖权"，另一方面以"被告人在
西班牙境内"作为前提。2018 年 12 月，在对 2014 年立法全面的宪
法审查中，西班牙宪法法院认为：不能从联大、国际法院或欧洲人
权法院的陈述中推断出，存在一项由缔约国强制执行的、绝对和一
般性的普遍管辖权原则。在这方面，不能依据《宪法》第 24 条第 1
款，主张 2014 年《司法权力组织法》第 23 条第 4 款规定了纯粹的
普遍关注型管辖权原则。[24] 由此可见，纯粹的普遍关注型管辖权的
实践在西班牙也落下了帷幕。

## 3. 阿根廷

近年来，阿根廷有关普遍管辖权的立法和司法实践比较积极。

---

23　2009 年 11 月，西班牙颁布《第 1/2009 号组织法》，对普遍管辖权进行了重大改革：第
一，第 23 条第 4 款第 1 项增加反人类罪。第二，第 23 条第 4 款第 8 项修改为："根据国际公约和
条约，特别是关于国际人道法和保护人权的公约，应当在西班牙追诉的其他犯罪。"第三，在第
23 条第 4 款列举罪名后新增两款条文："在不损害西班牙签署的国际公约和条约规定的前提下，
为使西班牙法院对上述罪行行使管辖权，必须确定被指控的行为人在西班牙境内，或受害人中有
西班牙公民，或案件与西班牙有其他联系，并且在任何情况下，其他有管辖权的国家或国际法院
未启动相关程序，包括对这些罪行开展有效的调查和起诉。在确定前款提及的国家或法院已对被
指控行为启动相关程序的情况下，西班牙法院应暂停提起刑事诉讼。"2014 年 3 月，西班牙颁布
《第 1/2014 号组织法》，对《司法权力组织法》第 23 条第 4 款进行大幅修改，主要体现为：第
一，改变了过去第 23.4 条列举罪名的立法模式，详细规定了不同罪行适用的不同前提条件。第
二，废除了 2009 年"与西班牙相关联"的兜底性规定，穷尽列举了每项罪行适用的关联因素。
第三，补充了新类型的关联因素，提高了"与西班牙相关联"的紧密程度要求，例如行为人现身
西班牙境内不再单独作为适用条件。第四，将补充性原则单独规定为第 23 条第 5 款，缩小其适用
范围而提高了灵活性。

24　"Sentencia 140/2018, de 20 de diciembre de 2018," Tribunal Constitucional De España, Spain,
December 20, 2018, accessed June 8, 2023, http://hj.tribunalconstitucional.es/es/Resolucion/Show/25823.

在立法上，普遍管辖权原则的依据最早见于 1994 年《阿根廷宪法》第 118 条。该条规定，"所有非由众议院享有的弹劾权引起的普通刑事案件，陪审团一经设立，应由陪审团决定。审判应在犯罪发生的省份进行；但如果是在国境外违反国际公法的案件，应在国会以特别法确定的地点进行审判"。[25]在提交给联大第六委员会第 73 届和第 77 届会议的答复中，阿根廷援引了宪法第 118 条表明其接受普遍管辖原则，[26] 并将该条作为对灭绝种族罪、反人类罪、战争罪、酷刑罪、强迫失踪罪等罪行适用普遍管辖的国内法律依据。[27]

在普遍管辖权的具体适用上，阿根廷不要求被告人"现身"境内，而强调普遍管辖原则的附属性和补充性，即如果该罪行此前未被当局或国际法庭起诉，那么阿根廷便可以启动调查，从而行使普遍管辖权。因此，阿根廷理论上拥有相当广泛和宽松的普遍管辖权。

在普遍管辖权的实践方面，阿根廷近年来相当活跃。阿根廷于 2010 年适用普遍管辖权原则，审理了 1939—1975 年佛朗哥统治期间在西班牙犯下的罪行。这个过程看似阿根廷对西班牙在 2005 年破例对一阿根廷前官员阿道夫·希林格（Adolfo Scilingo）行使管辖权

---

25　Constitución de la Nación Argentina, Ley N°: 24. 430, Argentina, 1994, art. 118, accessed June 8, 2023, http://servicios. infoleg. gob. ar/infolegInternet/anexos/0-4999/804/norma. htm.

26　《关于普遍管辖权原则的范围和适用秘书长的报告》，联合国大会第六委员会第 73 届会议，A/73/123，第 2 页（"第 73 届联大会议报告"）；《关于普遍管辖权原则的范围和适用秘书长的报告》，联合国大会第六委员会第 77 届会议，A/77/186（"第 77 届联大会议报告"），第 2 页。

27　第 77 届联大会议报告，第 18—26 页。

的一种反应措施，[28] 但后来在人权机构、非政府组织的推动下得到扩大，而且来势凶猛。不久，阿根廷在 2014 年审理了以色列在加沙地区犯下的反人类罪案件。[29] 2018 年 11 月，人权观察组织（Human Rights Watch）向阿根廷联邦法院起诉沙特阿拉伯王储穆罕默德·本·萨勒曼（Mohammed bin Salman），要求阿根廷适用宪法第 118 条的普遍管辖权原则，对其"在也门代理人战争中犯下的反人类罪"和"可能参与卡舒吉遇害案"展开调查。阿根廷联邦法官阿里尔·莱霍（Ariel Lejo）办公室要求阿根廷外交部从也门、土耳其和国际刑事法院收集相关指控的信息。[30] 2021 年 11 月，英国缅甸罗兴亚组织（BROUK）及六名女性受害者依据普遍管辖权原则向布宜诺斯艾利斯法院起诉，指控缅甸军方对罗兴亚人的"持续的种族灭绝"，并获得立案。[31] 2023 年 6 月 7 日，罗兴亚人首次在布宜诺斯艾利斯出庭。[32] 值得注意的是，2021 年 6 月，某些非政府组织利用阿

---

28　María Manuel Márquez Velásquez, "The Argentinian Exercise of Universal Jurisdiction 12 Years After its Opening," Opinio Juris, February 4, 2022, https://opiniojuris. org/2022/02/04/the-argentinian-exercise-of-universal-jurisdiction-12-years-after-its-opening/.

29　"Argentine court hears allegations of genocide against Myanmar leaders," RFA, June 7, 2023, accessed June 8, 2023, https://www. rfa. org/english/news/myanmar/rohingya-argentina-06072023162250. html.

30　《人权观察：继阿根廷后，将在其他国家继续起诉沙特王储》，2018 年 11 月 29 日，https://chinese. aljazeera. net/news/2018/11/29/watch-will-pursue-binsalman-in-other-countries-after-argentina，访问日期：2023 年 6 月 25 日。

31　"Historic Decision By Argentinian Courts To Take Up Genocide Case Against Myanmar," November 28, 2021, accessed June 25, 2023, https://www. brouk. org. uk/historic-decision-by-argentinian-courts-to-take-up-genocide-case-against-myanmar/.

32　《罗兴亚难民亲赴阿根廷法院亲身揭露军方暴行》，2023 年 6 月 8 日，https://atvnewsonline. com/asean/251750/，访问日期：2023 年 6 月 25 日。

根廷宪法普遍管辖权原则向阿根廷联邦刑事法院起诉，以所谓"种族灭绝罪"和"反人类罪"对中国官员发起指控。[33] 看来，在比利时、西班牙的"纯粹的普遍关注"型管辖权帷幕落下之后，寻求阿根廷法院行使普遍管辖权成为原告的一个选择。

### 4. 其他国家

以色列、葡萄牙等国家也存在着纯粹的普遍关注型管辖权的实践。不过或由于背景特殊，或由于范围有限，其他国家的实践未如比利时、西班牙那样引起重视。其中，以色列的普遍管辖实践一般集中在对二战战争犯罪的追诉方面。以色列有关普遍管辖权的主要立法包括《纳粹与勾结纳粹（惩罚）法》《防止和惩治灭绝种族法》等。《纳粹与勾结纳粹（惩罚）法》第 1 条明确指出：本法主要是适用于在纳粹政权下的敌国[34]（enemy country）犯下"反犹太人罪""反人类罪"和"战争罪"的任何人。第 9 条则规定：犯有本法规定的罪行的人，即使他已经在国外（包括国际法庭或仲裁庭）受审，也可以在以色列受到审判。[35]《防止和惩治灭绝种族法》则规定，在以色列境外实施本法规定的犯罪行为的人，可在以色列

---

33　"UHRP and WUC to Submit Universal Jurisdiction Complaint to the Criminal Courts of Argentina for Genocide & Crimes against Humanity against the Uyghur People, " UHRP, December 14, 2021, accessed June 25, 2023, https://uhrp. org/statement/uhrp-and-wuc-to-submit-universal-jurisdiction-complaint-to-the-criminal-courts-of-argentina/.

34　"敌国"是指纳粹德国及其他轴心国、任何部分或全部处于轴心国统治下的被占领土。

35　*Nazis and Nazi Collaborators ( Punishment) Law*, Art. 1. and Art. 9.

受到起诉和惩罚，就像他在以色列实施该行为一样。[36]

在司法实践中，"艾希曼案"（Eichmann Case）是受到世界关注的案件。以色列法院指出，"以色列有权制定这样的法律。[37] 由于相应犯罪攻击的是整个人类，属于严重违反国际法，在缺乏一个国际法庭审判的背景下，国际法非但不限制国家行使管辖权，反而需要每个国家的立法和司法机关采取行动，展开对相关罪犯的审判。在国际法上，审理这些犯罪的管辖权是普遍性的"。[38]

葡萄牙对计算机和通信欺诈罪、危害国家独立和完整罪、恐怖主义犯罪等罪行行使纯粹的普遍关注管辖权。结合葡萄牙刑法第5条和葡萄牙根据联大决议提交的资料，葡萄牙刑法在以下情况下可适用于境外犯罪：任何人实施的"计算机和通信欺诈罪"、"伪造货币、信用证书和封存价值物"和"伪造模具、重量和等价物"类犯罪、"危害国家独立和领土完整"类犯罪、"违反法治进程"和"违反选举"类犯罪、恐怖主义犯罪，以及恐怖组织犯下的特定罪行。在提交给联大资料的说明中，葡萄牙指出，上述所列罪行是"涉及葡萄牙法律确立的绝对的普遍管辖权的罪行"。[39] 不过，葡萄牙的普遍管辖实践所针对的罪行范围有限，甚至并未纳入一些违反国际人道法的罪行。

---

36　*The Crime of Genocide (Prevention and Punishment) Law*, Art. 5.

37　即《纳粹与勾结纳粹（惩罚）法》。

38　*International Law Reports*, Vol. 36, 1968, pp. 20-22.

39　Portugal, in UNGA, Sixth Committee, Sixty-fifth session, October 4, 2010, p. 2, accessed on June 8, 2023, https://www.un.org/en/ga/sixth/65/ScopeAppUniJuri_StatesComments/Portugal.pdf.

此外，在土耳其[40]、伊拉克[41]等国的法律中，也有部分条款接近于纯粹的普遍关注型管辖权，但是却基本上未曾真正行使，因而并未得到国际社会的关注。

## （二）普遍关注加现身型管辖权

美国、德国和澳大利亚是普遍关注加现身型管辖权的典型代表。此种类型管辖权的特点在于要求被告现身于行使管辖权的国家，尽管对于现身的条件——如现身的时间——并未形成一致意见，但毕竟由于现身而实现了一定的联系，从而其争议性较"纯粹的普遍关注"型管辖权为小。而且，普遍关注加现身型管辖权更加符合一些国家在刑事判决中不允许缺席审判的程序性要求，近年来的发展似乎呈上升趋势。

### 1. 美国

美国在刑事诉讼和民事诉讼中都涉及普遍管辖权的问题。其中，在刑事诉讼方面，美国刑事普遍管辖权法规一般要求被告位于或在美国被发现，因为美国的实践不允许缺席刑事审判。比如，美

---

40　土耳其《刑法典》第13条的规定体现了"纯粹的普遍关注型管辖权"："（1）土耳其法律应适用于在外国犯下的下列罪行，无论是否由土耳其公民或非公民犯下：a）第二卷第一章中定义的罪行。即反人类罪、种族灭绝。——笔者注

41　《伊拉克高级刑事法院规约》第1条第2款规定了伊拉克高级刑事法院的管辖权，体现了"纯粹的普遍关注型管辖权"："对被指控在1968年7月17日至2003年5月1日在伊拉克共和国或其他地方犯下本法第11条（灭绝种族罪）、第12条（反人类罪）、第13条（战争罪）和第14条（违反伊拉克法律）所列任何罪行的每个自然人，无论是伊拉克居民还是非伊拉克居民，包括以下罪行：灭绝种族罪、反人类罪、战争罪以及违反本法第14条所列伊拉克法律的行为。"

国早就建立了对海盗罪的普遍管辖，同样要求现身的因素，"任何人在公海犯下国际法所定义的海盗罪，随后被带入美国或在美国被发现，均应被终身监禁"。[42] 此外，美国还对奴隶制和奴隶贸易、种族灭绝、酷刑等实施普遍管辖。[43]

不过，对于一些得到较多共识的行使普遍管辖权的情形，美国并未全部纳入普遍管辖的范围，比如反人类罪和战争罪。美国并未制定有关反人类罪的联邦立法，而美国的战争罪的被告范围仅限美国人或美国武装部队成员。[44]

另外，对于恐怖主义犯罪和麻醉品贸易犯罪是否适用普遍管辖权，联邦法院之间存在争议。[45] 同样，联邦法院对于《海上禁毒执法法》（*Maritime Drug Law Enforcement Act*）是否创立了对海上麻醉品贸易的普遍管辖权存在争议。[46]

尽管对于民事诉讼中能否适用普遍管辖权或能否称之为普遍管辖权存在争议，但有观点认为《外国人侵权法》（*Alien Tort Statute*）

---

[42]  18 U. S. C. § 1651.

[43]  The American Law Institute, *Restatement of the Law Fourth, The Foreign Relations Law of the United States, Selected Topics in Treaties, Jurisdiction, and Sovereign Immunity*（St. Paul: American Law Institute Publishers, 2018）, p. 162.

[44]  Ibid.

[45]  比如在"尤瑟夫案"中，联邦第二巡回上诉法院的判决中称："恐怖主义不能提供普遍管辖的基础。"参见 *United States v Yousef*, 327 F. 3d 56, 107（2d Cir. 2003）。但是，在"尤尼斯案"中，华盛顿特区巡回上诉法院则表示："劫持飞行器很可能是国际法所明确谴责的少数几种犯罪之一，对该罪行国家可以实施普遍管辖权以审判犯罪嫌疑人，即使国家与劫机行为没有领土联系，且不涉及其公民。"参见 *United States v Yunis*, 924 F. 2d 1086, 1092（D. C. Cir. 1991）。

[46]  The American Law Institute, *Restatement of the Law Fourth, The Foreign Relations Law of the United States, Selected Topics in Treaties, Jurisdiction, and Sovereign Immunity*（St. Paul: American Law Institute Publishers, 2018）, pp. 161-162.

和《酷刑受害者保护法》（*Torture Victim Protection Act*）使联邦法院能够对于人权诉讼行使一定的民事方面的普遍管辖权。

《外国人侵权法》主要目的是保护人权，该法赋予联邦法院对酷刑、法外处决、强迫失踪、反人类罪、残忍、不人道或有辱人格的待遇、长期任意拘留、种族灭绝、战争罪、奴隶制、国家资助的性暴力和强奸为案由的民事侵权诉讼案件的管辖权。该法有关诉讼中的被告人国籍不限，但必须现身在美国，并且必须在侵犯人权的行动中以官方身份出现或者是依据法律要求行事。

《酷刑受害者保护法》相比于外国人侵权法案中管辖的罪名较少，只包括酷刑和法外处决，并且只有自然人可以成为被告，而且要求原告已经穷尽了侵权行为发生国的救济手段，而被告必须是以官方身份行事或者给予他人官方身份的印象来行事。[47]

总体而言，美国在民事方面的普遍管辖权实践较为特殊，为跨国人权诉讼提供了机会。应当注意的是，在美国，现任外国国家元首、外交部长或具有外交豁免权的官员一般在诉讼中享有豁免。然而，一旦他们离任，无论是国家元首，还是其他官员，即使是因任职期间犯下的侵权行为也可能成为人权民事诉讼的被告。此外，无论是刑事方面还是民事方面的普遍管辖权，美国的实践一般要求被告必须出现在美国境内，因此可以认为美国行使的是"普遍关注加现身型管辖权"。

---

[47] Torture Victim Protection Act note of 1991, Sec. 2, accessed June 8, 2023, https://www.govinfo.gov/content/pkg/STATUTE-106/pdf/STATUTE-106-Pg73.pdf.

## 2. 德国

近年来，德国是行使普遍管辖权比较活跃且在该方面受到高度关注的国家。德国主要通过《国际刑法典实施法》确立起普遍关注加现身型管辖权。此法第 1 条指出：本法应适用于本法指定的所有违反国际法的严重刑事犯罪，即使犯罪是在国外发生的，与德国无关。[48]《国际刑法典实施法》详细列举了德国法院可以行使普遍管辖权的罪名，包括灭绝种族罪（第 6 条）、反人类罪（第 7 条）、危害个人的战争罪（第 8 条）、危害财产和其他权利的战争罪（第 9 条）、危害人道主义行动和标志的战争罪（第 10 条）、涉及使用被禁止的作战手段罪（第 11 条、第 12 条）[49] 实践中，德国适用《国际刑法典实施法》作出有罪判决的大部分案例与卢旺达大屠杀和前南斯拉夫内战有关，且被告均具备"现身德国"的特征。不过，近年来德国也开始关注叙利亚等地发生的国际罪行。

此外，德国《刑法典》在第 6 条规定，"本法适用于在德国境外实施的受国际保护的法律利益"，具体而言包括下列行为：涉及核能、爆炸物及辐射的罪行，攻击空中和海上交通工具，以性剥削为目的或以工作剥削为目的的人口贩运和协助人口贩运，非法毒品交易，传播色情物品，伪造货币、证券及相关的准备行为，协助欺诈，根据对德国具有约束力的国际协定必须起诉的罪行。[50]

---

48　*Act to Introduce the Code of Crimes against International Law*, Sec. 1.

49　Ibid., Sec. 6-Sec. 12.

50　*The Criminal Law of Germany*, Sec. 6.

德国《刑事诉讼法》第 153 条第 6 款规定检察官在四种情况下可以酌定不起诉：没有德国人涉嫌犯罪，罪行不是针对德国人犯下的，被告不在德国，嫌疑人已经被犯罪地国、嫌疑人国籍国或受害人国籍国的法院追究。[51] 这似乎表明德国司法机构在行使普遍管辖权时会考虑一些额外的因素，而并非仅考虑相关罪行的普遍关注程度。

截至 2019 年 2 月，德国有 80 多项基于普遍管辖权原则的调查正在进行中，分属 11 个检察官，地域分布在非洲与中东地区，如叙利亚、伊拉克、利比亚、刚果等国。[52] 德国联邦检察官办公室自 2014 年 8 月 1 日以来一直在对"伊斯兰国"的相关成员进行结构性调查，理由是怀疑他们参与涉及种族灭绝行为。并下发两张逮捕令，其中一名犯罪嫌疑人被从希腊引渡到德国，并自 2020 年 4 月开始对其种族灭绝罪、反人类罪和战争罪指控进行审判。[53]

在叙利亚问题上，德国司法部门自 2011 年起就已经启动了针对叙利亚冲突的结构性调查，所涉罪名包括战争罪与反人类罪。德国科布伦茨高等地区法院分别在 2021 年 2 月 24 日与 2022 年 1 月 13 日判处一名叙利亚国民和一名前叙利亚情报官员犯有危害人类与共

---

51　*Code of Criminal Procedure of Germany*, Sec. 153（f）para. 2.

52　*Universal Jurisdiction Law and Practice in Germany*, 2019, accessed June 8, 2023, https://www.justiceinitiative.org/publications/universal-jurisdiction-law-and-practice-germany.

53　Pressestellee, Oberlandesgericht Frankfurt（OLG Frankfurt）, Beginn der Hauptverhandlung gegen Taha Al. J. 24, April 24, 2020, accessed June 8, 2023, https://ordentlichegerichtsbarkeit.hessen.de/pressemitteilungen/beginn-der-hauptverhandlung-gegen-taha-al-j.

谋反人类罪。[54] 此二人此前均已现身德国并已经在 2019 年被逮捕。[55]

综上所述，尽管德国近年来的普遍管辖权实践较为积极，但并未达到比利时和西班牙此前的程度。从立法和实践来看，德国的普遍管辖权行使前提要求被告现身于德国，因此并不是"纯粹的普遍关注型的管辖权"。

## 3. 澳大利亚

澳大利亚 1995 年《刑法》第 268 条规定了禁止种族灭绝罪、反人类罪和战争罪，第 274 条规定了禁止酷刑罪。所有这些罪行均适用于不受限制的 D 类管辖权，《刑法》第 15 条第 4 款将 D 类管辖权解释为：管辖权的适用不受构成被指控罪行的行为或构成被指控罪行的行为的结果是否发生在澳大利亚影响，不要求受害者或肇事者必须是澳大利亚公民、居民或法人团体。[56] 不过，有关案件仅仅会在被告出席的情况下进行。

为防止对第 268 条和第 274 条下的罪行提起不适当的起诉，通常需要获得总检察长的同意才能开始起诉。虽然同意规则因犯罪类型而异，但对于完全在澳大利亚境外发生的犯罪，始终需要总检察

---

54 《秘书长关于普遍管辖权原则范围和适用的报告》（第 76 届联合国大会），RES/A/76/203，第 6 页。

55 Anwar Raslan and Eyad Al Gharib, TRIAL International, accessed June 8, 2023, https://trialinternational. org/latest-post/anwar-raslan-and-eyad-al-gharib/.

56 "Information Submitted by Australia on the Scope and Application of the Principle of Universal Jurisdiction in Accordance with General Assembly Resolution 64/117," Derechos, accessed June 8, 2023, https://www. derechos. org/intlaw/doc/ausuj. html.

长的同意。总检察长在行使酌处权决定是否应进行起诉时，可能会考虑国际法、惯例、国际礼让，有关诉讼是否正在或可能在外国进行以及公共利益等因素。

澳大利亚是《日内瓦公约》《国际刑事法院规约》《禁止酷刑公约》《防止及惩治灭绝种族罪公约》等公约的缔约国，但是澳大利亚《刑法》规定的行使普遍管辖权的罪行范围并不限于条约规定，还包括了其他罪行，因此可以认为澳大利亚行使普遍管辖权的依据不仅限于条约。不过，澳大利亚对于普遍管辖权的案件不支持缺席审判，要求被告人必须现身于澳大利亚，因此澳大利亚行使的是普遍关注加现身型管辖权。

## （三）普遍关注加条约、现身型管辖权

从本质上讲，普遍关注加条约、现身型管辖权并非普遍管辖权，而是基于条约而行使的管辖权。一般来说，若国家批准了有关的国际条约，并依据条约在国内立法或实践中规定或行使条约所规定的管辖权，且要求被告现身于该国，则属于普遍关注加条约、现身型管辖权。英国和法国的有关实践属于此种类型。

### 1. 英国

英国是《日内瓦公约》《国际刑事法院规约》《禁止酷刑公约》《防止及惩治灭绝种族罪公约》的缔约国。为履行条约义务，英国通过了《日内瓦公约法》《国际刑事法院规约法》《种族灭绝法》

《战争罪法》等国内立法。以 1957 年《日内瓦公约法》为例，该法第 1 条规定：不论国籍、所在地是否在联合王国，只要实施、教唆、诱导他人作出违反本法的行为，都应当被认为犯下重罪并且应当被判处终身监禁或者不超过 14 年的有期徒刑；如果根据本条在联合王国境外犯下的罪行，可在联合王国任何地方对某人进行起诉、审判和惩罚，就如同该罪行是在该地方犯下的一样。

另外，根据英国发布的《关于调查和起诉可被普遍管辖罪行的说明》，对于酷刑和其他违反《日内瓦公约》的罪行的犯罪人，英格兰和威尔士地区的机构可以对现身于该地或者计划现身该地的人员启动调查和起诉程序；但是对于种族灭绝罪、战争罪和反人类罪，英格兰和威尔士法院只能对其国民或者居民行使管辖权。

"皮诺切特引渡案"在英国有关普遍管辖权的司法实践中是最受瞩目的案件。1998 年，英国地方法院应西班牙法官的请求下令拘捕了正在伦敦就医的皮诺切特，他被指控为涉嫌在任期内对西班牙公民及其后裔进行谋杀、施用酷刑和灭绝种族的罪行。英国法院认定皮诺切特因违反《禁止酷刑公约》的行为而不享有豁免权。[57]

综上所述，英国行使普遍管辖权的依据主要来自条约，而且在国内立法和司法实践中也明确了，犯罪人国籍和犯罪行为发生地不限，但要求其身处英国，因此属于普遍关注加条约、现身型管辖权。

---

57　该案的结局是鉴于 84 岁的皮诺切特糟糕的健康状况，英国内务大臣杰克·斯特劳（Jack Straw）命令将其释放。

## 2. 法国

法国的普遍管辖权的立法主要为以下三部法律：《刑事诉讼法》《95-1 号法案》和《96-432 号法案》。《刑事诉讼法》第 689 条第 1 款规定：根据下列条款所述的国际公约，任何在法国境外犯下这些条款所列任何罪行的人，如果在法国，可由法国法院起诉和审判。[58] 随后，本条第 2 款至第 14 款详细列举了可依据的公约，包括《禁止酷刑和其他残忍、不人道或有辱人格的待遇或处罚公约》和《罗马规约》。[59]《95-1 号法案》和《96-432 号法案》分别使法国法院得以管辖被前南斯拉夫问题国际刑事法庭或卢旺达问题国际刑事法庭判决有罪的被告，以上两个法案依据第 827 号和第 955 号安理会决议制定。法国在提交给秘书长的材料中也指出，"两项安理会决议使得法国法院（依据此法）的普遍管辖权受到属人原则、属时原则和属地原则的限制"。[60]

司法实践方面，2005 年，加尔省巡回法庭判处毛里塔尼亚一名公民 10 年监禁，并为每名受害者支付 15 000 欧元的赔偿金和利息，罪名是 1990—1991 年在毛里塔尼亚实施酷刑的行为。这是法国首次此类定罪。[61] 法国在司法实践中均要求被告具备"现身法国"这一要素。由此可见，法国承认的普遍管辖权是典型的普遍关注加条

---

58　*Code de procédure pénale*, Art. 689 (1).

59　Ibid., Art. 689 (2) and Art. 689 (11).

60　Permanent Mission of France to the United Nations, Ref: AT/sec No. 214, April 27, 2010, p. 4.

61　Ibid., p. 5.

约、现身型管辖权。

## （四）普遍关注加条约、现身并体制内属地或属人型
## 管辖权

普遍关注加条约、现身并体制内属地或属人型管辖权是一些国际条约所规定的，在条约体制内由缔约国行使的一种管辖权。这一情形属于典型的条约体制内部的协作事务，其意指，至少条约体制内的某一缔约国可以基于某一传统标准合法地行使管辖权，起诉国不过是在代替另一缔约国履行职责，不管该缔约国出于何种原因没有履行职责（如无能力管辖或不愿管辖）。这一条约体制实质上允许缔约国分享其传统的管辖权力，或者允许某一缔约国行使另一缔约国的管辖权。[62]《日内瓦公约》（1949）、《关于制止非法劫持航空器的公约》（1970）、《禁止并惩治种族隔离罪行国际公约》（1973）、《禁止酷刑和其他残忍、不人道或有辱人格的待遇或处罚公约》（1984），乃至《国际刑事法院罗马规约》（1998）等重要条约的有关条款都体现了这一条约体制。

比如，《禁止酷刑和其他残忍、不人道或有辱人格的待遇或处罚公约》第 5 条第 1 款和第 2 款规定如下：

1. 每一缔约国对下列情况中的罪行应采取一些必要的

---

62　易显河：《普遍管辖权的概念、逻辑和现状》，易显书译，《国际法学刊》2019 年第 1 期，第 117 页。

措施，以确立第 4 条中所述的管辖权：

（1）这种罪行发生在其管辖的任何领土内，或在该国注册的飞机或船只上；

（2）被指控的罪犯是该国国民；

（3）受害人是该国国民，而该国认为确系如此。

2. 每一缔约国同样应采取必要的措施，确立其对在下列情况中发生的罪行的管辖权：被指控的罪犯在该国管辖的任何领土内，该国不按第 8 条规定将他引渡至本条第 1 款所述的任何国家。

适用第 2 款的前提是，第 1 款必须已具潜在适用性，但被请求国不愿引渡被控犯罪嫌疑人。也就是说，犯罪嫌疑人或者被控罪行必须与某一缔约国（第 1 款所述之每一缔约国）之间存在基层的联系因素——领土、国籍或受害人国籍，以确立这一潜在适用性。由此，第 2 款所确立的就是一种普遍关注加条约、现身并体制内属地或属人管辖权。

国家根据其缔结的有关条约而在其国内法中规定条约体制内管辖权的情况很常见。比如，印度、新加坡、斯里兰卡等国通过《日内瓦公约法》以实施《日内瓦公约》。不过，正如前文所述，这种类型的管辖权已与真正的普遍管辖权的意旨相差甚远，实际上还存在管辖权行使的传统要素，只不过是在条约体系内分享而已。因此，此类管辖权在真正的普遍管辖权的发展方面价值有限。

# 三、结论

从普遍管辖权的国家实践情况来看，似乎国家对普遍管辖权的概念、范围和适用的认识和有关实践存在很大的混乱。甚至对于什么是普遍管辖权这一首要的问题都存在着南辕北辙的看法。本文根据有关的理论与实践，将普遍管辖权分为四类。但是，其中只有"纯粹的普遍关注"型管辖权才真正反映了普遍管辖权的意旨，才是真正意义的普遍管辖权。而其他几种则从本质上讲或可称为属地管辖，或可称为属人管辖，或来源于条约体制授权，并不是真正的普遍管辖。

## （一）普遍管辖权的国家实践发展情况

纯粹的普遍关注型管辖权的存在理由是为保护国际体系的权益，包括保护人权和对抗有罪不罚。鉴于国际社会缺乏世界政府，所以借由国家管辖权体系完成上述目标。然而纯粹的普遍关注型管辖权可能会侵犯国家主权平等原则，也可能被刻意滥用，从而使一些国家感到危险。在这样的情况下，纯粹的普遍关注型管辖权的发展注定坎坷，根本原因在于国际体系和国际法的现状。

我们发现，近年来，纯粹的普遍关注型管辖权的发展已经受挫。虽然在 20 世纪末到 21 世纪初，比利时、西班牙短暂地引领了一波普遍管辖权的发展高潮。然而，在其他国家施加的政治压力和国际法院的不利判决等因素影响下，两国已经放弃了纯粹的普遍关注型管辖权，甚至在行使基于现身或条约体制的管辖权时，还要比一些国家更加谨慎。

在比利时、西班牙的有关实践停滞的情况下，阿根廷反而"异军突起"。除了受理罗兴亚人案件外，还收到了有关中国官员的"种族灭绝罪"和"反人类罪"指控。这充分说明了普遍管辖权存在被以政治目的滥用的可能性。虽然目前针对中国的案件不太可能产生实际影响，但中国官员在外访阿根廷之前，提前考虑普遍管辖权的问题是有必要的。总之，上述有关实践发展情况说明，纯粹的普遍关注型管辖权远未形成习惯国际法。

德国虽然被一些人认为是普遍管辖权发展的后起之秀，但实际上德国行使的已不再是纯粹的普遍关注型管辖权，鉴于德国要求犯罪嫌疑人现身于德国。因此，准确地说，德国所行使的普遍管辖权应属于普遍关注加现身型管辖权。

普遍关注加现身型管辖权是与纯粹的普遍关注型管辖权最为接近的一种。当然，由于要求犯罪嫌疑人的现身，此种管辖权也可能被认定为一种属地管辖权。行使普遍关注加现身型管辖权的国家实践比较丰富，常常是由于有关国家不承认刑事审判可以缺席审判，所以在普遍关注的罪行的基础上增加了现身的条件。由于存在属地的要素，此种管辖权更可能为其他国家所接受。美国所行使的普遍管辖权也一般是此种。不过，值得注意的是，虽然存在争议，但是美国似乎在民事方面也行使一定的普遍管辖权，即通过《外国人侵权法》等对于侵犯人权的外国被告行使管辖，而且在一些司法实践中发现，离任的外国国家官员在一些有关侵犯人权的民事诉讼中无法因为在职期间的某些行为享有豁免。

普遍关注加条约、现身型管辖权和普遍关注加条约、现身并体制内属地或属人型管辖权都基于条约，后者适用范围较窄，增加了"体制内属地或属人"的条件。在这两种情况下，"普遍关注"这一真正的普遍管辖权的核心要素甚至是多余的，所以与真正的普遍管辖权相差甚远。另外，由于条约是授权基础，围绕此种管辖权的争议是很少的。

## （二）中国与普遍管辖权

中国对普遍管辖权的立场十分谨慎，正如在向联大提交的有关普遍管辖权问题的声明中所表示的，"一国管辖权的确立应当以该国与所涉案件之间存在有效和充分的联系因素为前提条件，并应将其限于一个合理的范围"。[63]

从实践来看，一般认为，中国《刑法》第9条规定了普遍管辖的原则。该条明确规定："对于中华人民共和国缔结或者参加的国际条约所规定的罪行，中华人民共和国在所承担条约义务的范围内行使刑事管辖权的，适用本法。"在程序方面，行使《刑法》第9

---

63　China, *Information from and Observations by China on the Scope and Application of the Principle of Universal Jurisdiction*, 2010, http://www. un. org/en/ga/sixth/65/ScopeAppUniJuriStatesComments/China. pdf, accessed June 8, 2023. 作为例外，中国承认习惯国际法早已确立各国有权对发生在管辖区域之外的海盗行为进行惩治。中国政府在同一文件中有此表态。

条规定的普遍管辖权的条件是被指称的犯罪人出现在中国境内。[64] 由此可见，中国的普遍管辖权必须基于条约，而根据缔结条约的不同，中国可能行使的是普遍关注加条约、现身型管辖权或普遍关注加条约、现身并体制内属地或属人型管辖权。因此，中国实际上并没有建立起真正的普遍关注型管辖权体系。另外，中国尚未把本国缔结或者参加的国际条约中的罪行都规定在刑法分则中，使其成为国内法上的罪行，由此在行使基于条约的管辖权时还可能存在违反"法无明文不为罪"原则等较大障碍。

在应对其他国家行使普遍管辖权方面，总体来说，我们应该关注的是纯粹的普遍关注型管辖权和普遍关注加现身型管辖权，这两种管辖权才具备更大的意义或风险。目前来看，虽然纯粹的普遍关注型管辖权相较此前来说较少出现，但德国、美国等国家在普遍关注加现身型管辖权方面较为活跃，有关实践较为丰富。当然，普遍管辖权的行使可能不只是一个法律问题，也常常与国内政策、政治背景、国家力量等有关，由此，在中美大国博弈的时代背景下，在某些情况下，特别是对于离任国家高级官员来说，避免其现身于美国可能是有必要的。

综上所述，从国家实践来看，显然纯粹的普遍关注型管辖权总体上处于衰退趋势，尽管存在一些波折和不确定，而普遍关注加现身型管辖权的发展情况似乎比较稳健。有学者认为，普遍关注加现身型管辖权可能作为一个替代品。不过，普遍关注加现身型管辖权

---

64　高铭暄主编《新编中国刑法学》上，中国人民大学出版社，1998，第53页。

并不是真正的普遍管辖权，而且有关国家实践证据尚不足以充分证明普遍关注加现身型管辖权的习惯国际法规则业已形成。

至于普遍管辖权的未来发展趋势，鉴于其根基在于国际体系的现状，可能在短期内不会发生太大的变化。不过，从长期来看，纯粹的普遍关注型管辖权可能存在发展空间。原因是普遍管辖权的概念和逻辑合乎情理，其所针对的罪行侵犯了国际社会整体的基本价值，其在一定意义上可成为国际体系维护其权益的强有力武器。另外，纯粹的普遍关注型管辖权的意旨契合当前国际法出现的对"共同利益"的追求与保护的发展趋势，在审慎、严格地运用下也许能够在未来得到一定发展。

# 涉普遍关注型管辖权的主要国家实践情况选编

董健宁　汪鑫宇　金凛　林芝羽　李介豪

## 编写人员内容分配情况

董健宁：西班牙、葡萄牙、拉丁美洲、比利时

汪鑫宇：比利时、法国

金　凛：非洲、亚洲部分国家、德国

林芝羽：英国、美国、大洋洲

李介豪：亚洲部分国家、法国、德国、俄罗斯

# 目　录

# 一、欧洲

欧洲各国，尤其是西欧的比利时、西班牙与德国等国家，具有比较前沿的普遍管辖权的司法制度与实践。在实践方面，比利时与西班牙都有依据普遍管辖权起诉他国领导人之先例，而德国常年深耕于对中东、非洲各国国际罪行的调查，具备丰富的理论与司法判例。因此，本部分以此为重点，展开梳理与论述。

## （一）比利时

目前，比利时在普遍管辖权的行使方面，主要体现了普遍关注加条约、现身型管辖权。对于"现身"要件，比利时要求"被告人在比利时有主要居所"，立场较为严格。尽管如此，比利时曾一度走在行使普遍管辖权的最前沿，起诉了美国总统布什（George Walker Bush）、以色列总理沙龙（Ariel Sharon）、刚果（金）外交与国际合作国务部长耶罗迪亚（Abdulaye Yerodia Ndombasi）等多名重要人物。总体而言，比利时经历了由"纯粹的普遍关注"型向"普遍关注加条约、现身"型管辖权转变的过程。

2003 年前，比利时属于"纯粹的普遍关注"型管辖权，被认为"拥有着世界上范围最广泛的普遍管辖权法律"。[1] 1993 年 6 月，为

---

[1]    Malvina Halberstam, "Belgium's Universal Jurisdiction Law: Vindication of International Justice or Pursuit of Politics?" *Cardozo Law Review*, 25, no. 1 (2003): 247.

履行 1949 年《日内瓦公约》及其附加议定书义务，比利时通过《关于惩罚严重违反 1949 年 8 月 12 日日内瓦公约及 1977 年 6 月 8 日附加议定书罪行法》，根据该法，任何犯有战争罪的犯罪嫌疑人都可以在比利时被起诉，而不论其国籍、被害人国籍、犯罪时间和犯罪地点，也不论该人是否现身比利时境内，[2] 体现了"缺席的普遍管辖"原则（universal jurisdiction in absentia），并成立专门负责调查国际罪行的机构。[3] 该法赋予了比利时法院极为广泛的权限，正因为管辖权的范围如此之大，该法被称为《万国管辖权法》。

1999 年 2 月，比利时议会对《万国管辖权法》进行了修订，该法案被更名为《关于惩罚严重违反国际人道法罪行的法》，此次修订进一步拓展了《万国管辖权法》的适用范围，将普遍管辖的罪行扩大到灭绝种族罪和反人类罪，同时规定犯罪嫌疑人不能够主张任何种类的豁免。[4] 由此，比利时建立起当时最为激进的"绝对的普遍管辖权"。在适用范围极其广泛的法律下，"大量的案件如雪花般飞来"，当时比利时法院已经登记了包括伊拉克总统萨达姆、古巴国务委员主席卡斯特罗、巴勒斯坦领袖阿拉法特、乍得总统哈布雷、智利前总统皮诺切特等在内的许多案件。[5]

---

2　Stijin Deklerck（涂建平）：《普遍性管辖原则：比利时的〈反暴行法〉》，朱利江译，《北大国际法与比较法评论》2004 年第 4 期，第 296 页。

3　Wolfgang Kaleck, "From Pinochet to Rumsfeld: Universal Jurisdiction in Europe 1998–2008," *Michigan Journal of International Law*, no. 3（2009）: 932.

4　Stijin Deklerck（涂建平）：《普遍性管辖原则：比利时的〈反暴行法〉》，朱利江译，《北大国际法与比较法评论》2004 年第 4 期，第 296—297 页。

5　Roozbeh（Rudy）B. Baker, "Universal Jurisdiction and the Case of Belgium: A Critical Assessment," *ILSA Journal of Int'l & Comparative Law* 16, no. 1（2009,）: 149–163.

2001 年 4 月，在比利时第一起依据《万国管辖权法》提起的"四名布塔雷人案"（the Butare Four Case）中，四名向比利时申请难民的卢旺达人被控灭绝种族罪，分别被判处 12 年至 20 年有期徒刑。[6] 由于卢旺达及卢旺达特别法庭均未提出引渡要求，案件进展十分顺利，并加快了比利时行使普遍管辖权的步伐。2001 年 6 月，在沙龙案（Sharon Case）中，比利时法院根据受害者指控对以色列总理沙龙（Ariel Sharon）和国防部长亚隆（Amos Yaron）启动调查程序。2002 年 6 月，比利时上诉法院裁决确认了 1993 年、1999 年有关普遍管辖权法律的效力，但援引 1878 年《刑事诉讼法》第 12 条，认为只有当被告人"出现"在比利时境内时，才能行使普遍管辖权而撤销案件。2003 年 2 月，比利时最高法院在裁决中认为 1878 年《刑事诉讼法》第 12 条并不要求被告在比利时境内，即使沙龙不在比利时，比利时也有权对沙龙提起诉讼，但在随后的诉讼程序中以"国家豁免"为由将案件撤销。[7]

2002 年 2 月，国际法院就刚果（金）诉比利时逮捕令案作出判决，认定比利时于 2000 年签发针对刚果（金）外交部长耶罗迪亚（Abdulaye Yerodia Ndombasi）战争罪及反人类罪的逮捕令侵犯国家豁免原则。[8] 虽然国际法院没有处理刚果（金）提出的"行使缺席

---

6　Luc Reydams, "Belgium's First Application of Universal Jurisdiction: The Butare Four Case," *Journal of International Criminal Justice,* no. 1（2003）: 433–434.

7　"Judgment of the Court of Cassation of Belgium in the Sharon & Yaron Case," February 12, 2003, accessed June 8, 2023, https://www.derechos.org/intlaw/doc/belsharon.html.

8　Arrest Warrant of 11 April 2000（*Democratic Republic of the Congo v Belgium*）, Judgment, *ICJ Reports,* 2002.

的普遍管辖违反国际法"问题，但判决结果无疑是压垮比利时纯粹的普遍关注型管辖权的"最后一根稻草"。

2003 年，比利时议会对《万国管辖权法》进行了两次修改，使得比利时放弃纯粹的普遍关注型管辖权，转向普遍关注加条约、现身型管辖权。在修订过程中，众议院司法委员会的大多数委员认为，通过向比利时法院提交无确凿证据或政治动机明显的案件，有关普遍管辖权的法律已经被滥用。[9] 根据 2003 年 4 月修订后的《万国管辖权法》，只有在被告人和比利时存在以下联系时，受害人才可以提起诉讼：（1）被告人位于比利时境内；（2）犯罪发生在比利时境内；（3）受害人为比利时公民或已经在比利时连续居住满三年，否则只能由比利时国家检察机关提起公诉。同时规定，只有在国际法允许下的情况下，才可以不考虑豁免事宜。[10] 虽然修订后的法律大大限制了适用普遍管辖的条件，但仍保留了"缺席的普遍管辖权"的一般原则，因此拥有广泛管辖权的比利时所面临的政治压力并未减轻。

2003 年 3 月的布什案（Bush Case）再次将《万国管辖权法》推向风口浪尖。受害人向比利时法院起诉，指控美国前总统布什（George Herbert Walker Bush）、副总统切尼（Richard Bruce Cheney）、国务卿鲍威尔（Colin Luther Powell）等在 1991 年海湾战争期间犯下

---

9　Stijn Deklerck（涂建平）：《普遍性管辖原则：比利时的〈反暴行法〉》，朱利江译，《北大国际法与比较法评论》2004 年第 4 期，第 296—297 页。

10　Roozbeh B. Baker, "Universal Jurisdiction and the Case of Belgium: A Critical Assessment," *ILSA Journal of International and Comparative Law* 16, no. 1（2009）: 155-157.

战争罪行。[11] 2003 年 6 月，美国国防部长拉姆斯菲尔德表示，如果比利时不彻底废除这部法律，那么美国将不得不把北约总部撤出布鲁塞尔。[12] 迫于政治压力，比利时政府于 2003 年 8 月 5 日宣布废除《万国管辖权法》，将有关国际罪行和普遍管辖权的法律纳入《比利时刑法典》。至此，比利时有关普遍管辖权的专门立法，连同曾经的先锋立场和激进实践彻底落幕。此后，只有在被控犯有国际罪行的被告人是比利时公民或居民，或犯罪被害人是比利时人或在罪行发生时在比利时已经连续居住达三年，或条约要求比利时进行管辖的前提下，比利时法院才有权行使管辖权。[13]

结合《比利时刑法典》第 136 条和 2010 年比利时向联大第六委员会提交的材料，国际罪行主要包括灭绝种族罪、反人类罪、战争罪、恐怖主义犯罪、贩运人口罪、切割女性生殖器罪等。相比曾经比利时在普遍管辖权的立法及实践上所体现的无拘束性和绝对性，如今比利时法院在行使普遍管辖权时受到法律更明确、更严格的约束和限制。综上所述，目前比利时有关普遍管辖权的国家实践属于普遍关注加条约、现身型。由"孤独地走在极不稳定的阵营最前沿"到"比有些国家限制还要更多"的历史嬗变表明了普遍管辖权自我限制的内在逻辑，更启示了与国家主权、国家豁免、国际刑

---

11　*Justice* 1（2003）：433-434.

12　Arrêt de la Cour de cassation de Belgique dans l'affaire Sharon & Yaron, Belgium, February 12, 2003, accessed January 12, 2023.

13　"Universal Jurisdiction in Europe—The State of the Art, Human Rights Watch，" June 2006, accessed May 8, 2024, https://www.refworld.org/reference/themreport/hrw/2006/en/63206.

事合作等国际法议题间的复杂关系。

## （二）西班牙

根据分类，目前西班牙属于普遍关注加条约、现身型管辖权。考虑到西班牙曾经针对我国提起过行使所谓普遍管辖权的诉讼，[14] 因此有必要梳理阐明西班牙普遍管辖权类型的历史嬗变。总体而言，西班牙的普遍管辖权立场经历了纯粹的普遍关注型，纯粹的普遍关注型向普遍关注加条约、现身型过渡和普遍关注加条约、现身型三个阶段。

在 20 世纪至 21 世纪初期的第一阶段，西班牙被公认为采取了"绝对的普遍管辖权"（absolute universal jurisdiction），[15] 根据其立法和司法实践，这一时期西班牙属于第一种"纯粹的普遍关注"型管辖权。

西班牙最早有关普遍管辖权的立法见于 1985 年《司法权力组织法》第 23 条第 4 款，根据该条，"西班牙法院对于西班牙公民或者外国人在西班牙领域外实施的以下任一犯罪，同样享有管辖权：（1）灭绝种族罪；（2）恐怖主义犯罪；（3）海盗罪和劫持航空器罪；（4）伪造外国货币罪；（5）卖淫罪；（6）非法贩运精神药物、毒品和麻醉品罪；（7）根据国际公约或者条约应当在西班牙追诉的

---

14　《普遍管辖权原则的范围和适用秘书长的报告》（第 66 届联合国大会），A/66/93，第 14—17 页。

15　"Spain: Practice to Rule 157: Jurisdiction over War Crimes," IRCR, IHL Database, Customary IHL, accessed June 8, 2023, https://ihl-databases.icrc.org/en/customary-ihl/v2/rule157?country=es.

其他犯罪".[16] 从字面含义看，除了第 23 条第 5 款规定的一事不再理（*ne bis in idem*）原则的限制外，第 23 条第 4 款对于普遍管辖权的适用没有规定任何限制条件，是"世界上最自由的普遍管辖权法令".[17]

这一时期的司法实践也体现了西班牙法院对纯粹的普遍关注型管辖权的坚持。1998 年，西班牙高等法院在皮诺切特案（Pinochet Case）中指出："当西班牙法院适用第 23 条第 4 款时，并不构成对犯罪发生地国家主权的干涉，而是在针对国际犯罪行使西班牙的主权。西班牙有权根据普遍管辖原则，对那些属于国际罪行清单、并得到西班牙国内立法确认的犯罪行使管辖权。"[18] 在希林格和卡瓦洛案（Scilingo and Cavallo Case）中，西班牙高等法院重申了"因反人类罪的普遍适用性而行使普遍管辖权"的观点："某些具有强行法和普遍性质的行为被认为是违反国际法的罪行。实施这些行为的最先后果就是由全人类共同确认其犯罪性质，即使犯罪人国籍国或者犯罪发生地的国内法不加禁止……相反，全人类及所有国家在起诉和惩治这些罪行上有着同等的利益。为确保有效满足这种利益，

---

16　"The Scope and Application of the Principle of Universal Jurisdiction: Information Provided by Spain," United Nations General Assembly 66th session, Spain, June 20, 2011, last accessed June 8, 2023, https://www. un. org/en/ga/sixth/66/ScopeAppUniJuri _ StatesComments/Spain% 20（S% 20to% 20E）. pdf.

17　Fausto Pocar and Magali Maystre, "The Principle of Complementarity: A Means towards a More Pragmatic Enforcement of the Goal Pursued by Universal Jurisdiction?" in Morten Bergsmo（ed.）, *Complementarity and the Exercise of Universal Jurisdiction of Core International Crimes* [ Brussels: Torkel Opsahl Academic EPublisher（TOAEP）, 2010], p. 166.

18　Adjudication of Jurisdiction on Pinochet, Audiencia Nacional Juzgado Central De, Spain, December 3, 1998, accessed June 8, 2023, http://elclarin. cl/fpa/pdf/p_031298_en. pdf.

国际法赋予所有国家起诉这些罪行的管辖权（普遍管辖权）。"[19] 在上述裁判中，西班牙法院着重突出所涉犯罪的"受普遍关注"和"关乎全人类利益"，作为行使普遍管辖权的合法性前提。鉴于这一时期西班牙立法和司法均未提及普遍管辖权的适用条件或限制因素，而主张绝对的普遍管辖权，因此属于纯粹的普遍关注型管辖权。

在 21 世纪初至 2009 年的第二阶段，西班牙经历了从纯粹的普遍关注型向普遍关注加条约、现身型管辖权的过渡。这一时期西班牙的国家实践体现出以下特点：第一，司法先行于立法。虽然《司法权力组织法》第 23 条第 4 款没有大幅修订，但法院在解释和适用时已经呈现"相对化"的趋势，采用"与西班牙相关联"（relevant link with Spain）作为限制条件；第二，过渡并非一帆风顺。由于西班牙"高等法院—最高法院—宪法法院"的三级法院体系，普遍管辖权的适用在上下级法院间较为割裂，由绝对到有限的进程反复周折。

立法上，这一时期西班牙颁布了三部涉及普遍管辖权的法律：2003 年《关于与国际刑事法院合作的组织法》、2005 年《第 3/2005 号组织法》和 2007 年《第 13/2007 号组织法》。这些法律仅扩大了 1985 年《司法权力组织法》第 23 条第 4 款中适用普遍管辖权的犯

---

19　Texto completo de la Sentencia 16/2005, Audiencia Nacional Sala De Lo Penal Seccion Tercera, Spain, April 19, 2005, accessed June 8, 2023, http://www.derechos.org/nizkor/espana/juicioral/doc/sentencia.html#5.%20SOBRE%20LA%20APLICABILIDAD.

罪种类，但仍未明确适用条件。具体而言，第 23 条第 4 款新增了腐化未成年或无行为能力人、切割女性生殖器和走私贩卖人口罪。值得注意的是，根据《第 3/2005 年号组织法》，对切割女性生殖器罪适用普遍管辖须满足"行为人在西班牙境内"的前提条件，[20] 这在一定程度上体现了立法上态度的收紧。

与此同时在司法中，西班牙法院对第 23 条第 4 款的适用产生了"有限化"和"绝对化"的争论——这一点在危地马拉案（Guatemala Case）中体现得尤为明显。1999 年，诺贝尔和平奖获得者里戈韦塔·门楚·图姆（Rigoberta Menchú Tum）请求西班牙高等法院依据第 23 条第 4 款对危地马拉政府官员犯下的灭绝种族罪、酷刑罪、恐怖主义犯罪等行使普遍管辖权。2002 年 12 月，西班牙高等法院全庭裁定，由于不存在危地马拉法院不作为的证据，目前无法确认西班牙对该案拥有管辖权。[21] 2003 年 2 月，西班牙最高法院以 8 票对 7 票作出裁定，认为"案件与西班牙相关联"是法院适用普遍管辖的合法性要件，且"这种关联应达到与国际法已经承认的其他管辖标准同等重要的程度"。因此，西班牙法院只能对涉及西班牙籍受害

---

20　Contribution of Spain on the Topic "The Scope and Application of the Principle of Universal Jurisdiction," Ministry of Foreign Affairs and Cooperation, Spain, February 22, 2016, accessed June 8, 2023, https://www.un.org/en/ga/sixth/71/universal_jurisdiction/spain_e.pdf.

21　ROLLO APELACIÓN N°: 115/2000, Audiencia Nacional Sala De Lo Penal, Spain, December 2002, accessed June 8, 2023, https://www.asser.nl/upload/documents/20120412T022442-Guatemala_Audiencia_nacional_13-12-2000.pdf.

人的部分进行调查。[22] 而少数法官意见认为，对灭绝种族罪等严重国际罪行行使普遍管辖权是为了打击有罪不罚现象，西班牙应代表整个国际社会利益起诉和惩治这些罪行。[23] 然而在 2005 年 9 月，西班牙宪法法院推翻了最高法院裁定，恢复了"绝对的普遍管辖权"立场。宪法法院认为，国际法已将对关涉所有国家的国际罪行的追诉和惩治普遍化，普遍管辖权便是仅根据这些罪行的严重性质而适用的管辖权，无须以"与西班牙相关联"为前提条件，且无论从文义还是立法目的分析，第 23 条第 4 款都应被解释为绝对的普遍管辖权。因此，除一事不再理原则外，下级法院无权对其适用增加限制条件。[24] 最终，关于第 23 条第 4 款解释和适用的争论以宪法法院重申"绝对的普遍管辖权"立场告终。

虽然已经释法，但第 23 条第 4 款在实践中仍然产生了矛盾和争论。一方面，由于宪法法院裁判的约束力，下级法院在判决上必须与其保持一致，导致在这一阶段西班牙频频援引绝对的普遍管辖

---

22　Decision No. 327/2003: Decision of the Spanish Supreme Court concerning the Guatemala Genocide Case, Supreme Court Criminal Division, Spain, February 25, 2003, accessed June 8, 2023, http://www. derechos. org/nizkor/guatemala/doc/stsgtm. html.

23　The Dissenting Opinion, written by distinguished judges, Judge Joaquín Delgado García, Judge José Antonio Martín Pallín, Judge Cándido Conde-Pumpido Tourón, Judge José Antonio Marañon Chavarri, Judge Joaquín Giménez Garcia, Judge Andrés Martinez Arrieta and Judge Perfecto Andrés Ibañez concerning the appeal for annulment of genocide number 803/2001 ( Mayan genocide) , Supreme Court Criminal Chamber, Spain, February 25, 2003, accessed June 8, 2023, http://www. derechos. org/nizkor/guatemala/doc/stsgtm. html.

24　Sentencia 237/2005, de 26 de septiembre, Tribunal Constitucional De España, Spain, September 26, 2005, accessed June 8, 2023, https://ihl-databases. icrc. org/en/national-practice/decision-no-237-guatemala-genocide-case-constitutional-tribunal-26-september-2005? activeTab = national-implementation-of-ihl?title =&typeOfPractice =&state = 17916&language =&from =&to =&sort = country&order =&topic =.

权，起诉了布什六同党案（Bush 6 Case）、美国酷刑计划案（U.S. Torture Program case）、阿斯拉弗案（Asharf Case）等大量案件；[25] 另一方面，下级法院在判决论证过程中又对绝对的普遍管辖权进行了批驳和修正。2005 年 11 月，西班牙高等法院就第 23 条第 4 款发布决议指出："本条无论如何都不应解释为无论犯罪发生地、犯罪人或者被害人国籍国为何，均可以对本条规定的犯罪提起刑事诉讼，因为任何国家都不负有通过适用刑法，对世界上所有人和所有地方单方面建立秩序的职责。"[26] 2007 年 10 月，西班牙最高法院在希林格和卡瓦洛案二审判决中指出："较为明智的做法是将普遍管辖权建立在案件与国家利益相关联的基础上。"[27] 可见，这一时期西班牙的国家实践呈现出"下级法院主张有限化"与"宪法法院坚持绝对化"的割裂，考虑到裁判结果和国际趋势，西班牙法院已经认识到该法条存在的问题，进而寻求"案件与西班牙相关联"作为适用条件，成为 2009 年《司法权力组织法》修订的基础。由于 2009 年后西班牙采取普遍关注加条约、现身型管辖权，因此这一阶段可以视

---

25　Accountability for U. S. Torture: Spain, The Center for Constitutional Rights, April 27, 2009, accessed June 8, 2023, https://ccrjustice. org/home/what-we-do/our-cases/accountability-us-torture-spain.

26　Resolution of the Plenary Session of the National High Court's Criminal Chamber regarding the interpretation of the judgment by the Constitutional Court on Guatemala, on November 3, 2005, Quote from Claudia Jiménez, "Combating Impunity for International Crimes in Spain: From the Prosecution of Pinochet to the Indictment of Garzón," International Catalan Institute for Peace, Working Paper No. 2011/1, May 1, 2011, p. 17.

27　Sentencia N°: 798/2007, Tribunal Supremo Sala De Lo Penal, Spain, October 1, 2007, accessed June 8, 2023, http://www. derechos. org/nizkor/espana/juicioral/doc/sentenciats. html # Tribunal; See also in Ignacio de la Rasilla del Moral, "The Swan Song of Universal Jurisdiction in Spain," *International Criminal Law Review* 9 (2009): 783.

为纯粹的普遍关注型管辖权向普遍关注加条约、现身型管辖权类型的过渡。

2009 年后的第三阶段，西班牙放弃了对纯粹的普遍关注型管辖权的坚持，开始对普遍管辖权适用条件进行限制。随着 2009 年和 2014 年两次修法，西班牙对普遍管辖权的国家实践最终落成于普遍关注加条约、现身型管辖权。

这一阶段最主要的国家实践是《司法权力组织法》的两次修订。2009 年 11 月，西班牙颁布《第 1/2009 号组织法》，对普遍管辖权进行了重大改革：第一，第 23 条第 4 款第 1 项增加反人类罪；第二，第 23 条第 4 款第 8 项修改为"根据国际公约和条约，特别是关于国际人道法和保护人权的公约，应当在西班牙追诉的其他犯罪"；第三，在第 23 条第 4 款列举罪名后新增两款条文：

在不损害西班牙签署的国际公约和条约规定的前提下，为使西班牙法院对上述罪行行使管辖权，必须确定被指控的行为人在西班牙境内，或受害人中有西班牙公民，或案件与西班牙有其他联系，并且在任何情况下，其他有管辖权的国家或国际法院未启动相关程序，包括对这些罪行开展有效的调查和起诉。

在确定前款提及的国家或法院已对被指控行为启动相

关程序的情况下，西班牙法院应暂停提起刑事诉讼。[28]

上述第二点强调了普遍管辖权的国际条约依据，第三点明确了普遍管辖权的适用条件，即被告人现身、消极属人管辖或"案件与西班牙有其他联系"，同时还规定了普遍管辖权的补充性原则。据此，"普遍关注加条约、现身"型管辖权的雏形已经出现，但值得注意的是，此时立法仍保留了"与西班牙相关联"这一可自由裁量的兜底性规定。

2014 年 3 月，西班牙颁布《第 1/2014 号组织法》，[29] 对《司法权力组织法》第 23 条第 4 款进行大幅修改，主要体现为：第一，改变了过去第 23 条第 4 款列举罪名的立法模式，详细规定了不同罪行适用的不同前提条件；第二，废除了 2009 年"与西班牙相关联"的兜底性规定，穷尽列举了每项罪行适用的关联因素；第三，补充了新类型的关联因素，提高了"与西班牙相关联"的紧密程度要求，例如行为人现身西班牙境内不再单独作为适用条件；第四，将补充性原则单独规定为第 23 条第 5 款，缩小其适用范围而提高了灵活性。在对《第 1/2014 号组织法》修改普遍管辖权部分的解释性说明中，西班牙指出：

---

28　The Scope and Application of the Principle of Universal Jurisdiction: Information Provided by Spain, United Nations General Assembly 66th session, Spain, June 20, 2011, accessed June 8, 2023, https://www. un. org/en/ga/sixth/66/ScopeAppUniJuri_StatesComments/Spain%20（S%20to%20E）.pdf.

29　Organic Act No. 1/2014 of 13 March（Official Gazette No. 63 of 14 March 2014），Spain, March 13, 2014, accessed June 8, 2023, http://www. derechos. org/nizkor/espana/doc/esplopj. html.

自 2009 年改革生效至今已有四年，现实表明，如今普遍管辖权不能脱离国际法的限制和要求。将一国的管辖权扩张至境外，进入另一国主权范围，必须限于国际法规定的领域，西班牙必须在这些领域中履行其国际承诺。超出西班牙领土边界的管辖权必须通过授权它的国际条约来证明其合法性，这已是国际社会的共识……

为此，如今改革规定了西班牙管辖权可能增加的积极和消极限制：立法者必须以符合国际条约的方式确定西班牙司法系统可以起诉哪些在国外犯下的罪行，以及在何种情况和条件下。[30]

2009 年改革后，西班牙法院在布什六同党案、美国酷刑计划案的后续进展中体现了补充性原则的适用和对关联因素的要求，并依据修订后的第 23 条第 4 款提起了以色列军舰案（Israeli Warship Case）。相较于改革前的十余起大案，2009 年改革后西班牙行使普遍管辖权的情形有所减少。[31] 2018 年 12 月，在对 2014 年立法整体的宪法审查中，西班牙宪法法院认为：不能从联大、国际法院或欧

---

30　Ley orgánica 1/2014, de modificación de la Ley orgánica 6/1985 del Poder Judicial relativa a la justicia universal, Spain, March 13, 2014, accessed June 8, 2023, https://ihl-databases. icrc. org/en/national-practice/organic-law-12014-modifying-organic-law-61985-judicial-power-universal? activeTab = all-national-practice? title = &typeofPractice = &state = 17916&language = &from = &to = &sort = category&order = &topic = .

31　The Scope and Application of the Principle of Universal Jurisdiction: Information Provided by Spain, United Nations General Assembly 66th session, Spain, June 20, 2011, accessed June 8, 2023, https://www. un. org/en/ga/sixth/66/ScopeAppUniJuri_StatesComments/Spain%20（S%20to%20E）.pdf.

洲人权法院的陈述中推断出，存在一项由缔约国强制执行的、绝对和一般性的普遍管辖权原则。在这方面，不能依据《宪法》第24条第1款，主张2014年《司法权力组织法》第23条第4款规定了绝对的普遍管辖权原则。[32] 至此，西班牙彻底放弃曾经绝对的普遍管辖权理念，转向更符合实际也更普遍的有限的普遍管辖权。

综上所述，由于主张"依据国际法和国际条约行使普遍管辖权"且第23条第4款管辖的若干罪行中都将"被告人在西班牙境内"作为适用条件，因此，目前西班牙总体上可被归类为普遍关注加条约、现身型管辖权。从第一种转向第三种管辖权类型，西班牙的国家实践也反映出普遍管辖权议题在国际法领域从宽松到严格、从激进到审慎的发展历程。虽然曾有恢复2009年前有关普遍管辖权法律的呼声，[33] 但根据西班牙宪法法院2018年12月的判决，西班牙在一段时间内应会保持现状，不会重新寻求"绝对的普遍管辖权"，这意味着西班牙回归纯粹的普遍关注型管辖权的可能性微乎其微。

## （三）德国

德国通过《国际刑法典实施法》（以下简称《实施法》）确立起本国法院的普遍管辖权。此法第一条开宗明义地指出：本法应适

---

32　Sentencia 140/2018, de 20 de diciembre de 2018, Tribunal Constitucional De España, Spain, December 20, 2018, accessed June 8, 2023, http://hj. tribunalconstitucional. es/es/Resolucion/Show/25823.

33　"La ministra Delgado expone en el Congreso los siete ejes que guiarán su gestión al frente de Justicia," Ministerio De Justicia, Spain, July 11, 2018, accessed June 8, 2023, https://www. lamoncloa. gob. es/serviciosdeprensa/notasprensa/justicia/Paginas/2018/110718-delgado. aspx.

用于本法指定的所有违反国际法的严重刑事犯罪，即使犯罪是在国外发生的，与德国没有关系。[34]《实施法》详细列举了德国法院可以行使普遍管辖权的罪名，包括灭绝种族罪（第 6 条）、反人类罪（第 7 条）、危害个人的战争罪（第 8 条）、危害财产和其他权利的战争罪（第 9 条）、危害人道主义行动和标志的战争罪（第 10 条）、涉及使用被禁止的作战手段罪（第 11 条、第 12 条）。[35]

此外，德国《刑法典》在第 6 条规定"本法适用于在德国境外实施的受国际保护的法律利益"，具体而言包括下列行为：涉及核能、爆炸物及辐射的罪行、攻击空中和海上交通工具、以性剥削为目的或以工作剥削为目的的人口贩运和协助人口贩运、非法毒品交易、传播色情物品、伪造货币及证券及相关的准备行为、协助欺诈、根据对德国具有约束力的国际协定必须起诉的罪行。[36]

德国《刑事诉讼法》第 153 条第 6 款规定检察官在四种情况下可以酌定不起诉：没有德国人涉嫌犯罪；罪行不是针对德国人犯下的；被告不在德国；嫌疑人已经被犯罪地国、嫌疑人国籍国或受害人国籍国的法院追究。[37] 这表明德国司法机构在行使普遍管辖权时会考虑一些额外的连接因素，而并非仅考虑相关罪行的普遍关注程度。德国适用《国际刑法典实施法》作出有罪判决的大部分案例与卢旺达大屠杀和南斯拉夫内战有关，且被告均具备"现身德国"的

---

34　*Act to Introduce the Code of Crimes against International Law*, Sec. 1.

35　Ibid. , Sec. 6-Sec. 12. 其中，第 11 条和第 12 条的区别在于二者涉及的具体犯罪行为不同。第 12 条特指使用有毒武器、生化武器和使用射入人体后易变形的子弹三种犯罪行为。

36　*The Criminal Law of Germany*, Sec. 6.

37　*Code of Criminal Procedure of Germany*, Sec. 153 (f), para. 2.

特征。

截至 2019 年 2 月，德国有 80 多项基于普遍管辖权原则的调查正在进行中，分属 11 个检察官，地域分布在非洲与中东地区，如叙利亚、伊拉克、利比亚、刚果等国。[38] 德国联邦检察官办公室自 2014 年 8 月 1 日以来一直在对"伊斯兰国"的相关成员进行结构性调查，理由是怀疑他们参与涉及灭绝种族行为。并下发两张逮捕令，其中一名犯罪嫌疑人被从希腊引渡到德国，并自 2020 年 4 月开始对其灭绝种族罪、反人类罪和战争罪指控进行审判。[39]

德国同样是卢旺达问题的积极参与者。从 2011 年 5 月至 2015 年 9 月，德国联邦法院对卢旺达反政府武装"卢旺达解放民主力量"头目穆尔瓦纳夏卡（Murwanashyka）于刚果民主共和国东部犯下的 39 项战争罪行与 26 项反人类罪行进行了审理，最终他于 2018 年被判处有罪。另外，2015 年，德国美因河畔法兰克福高等地区法院认定一名卢旺达公民在 1994 年于卢旺达犯下灭绝种族罪，并判处其终身监禁。根据原《刑法》第 220 条第 1 款，另一名卢旺达公民作为共同犯罪人被判处共同实施灭绝种族罪。虽然他本人没有实施杀人行为，但法院认为他对该罪行的实施作出了重大贡献。[40]

---

38　*Universal Jurisdiction Law and Practice in Germany, 2019*, https://www.justiceinitiative.org/publications/universal-jurisdiction-law-and-practice-germany.

39　Pressestellee, Oberlandesgericht Frankfurt（OLG Frankfurt），Beginn der Hauptverhandlung gegen Taha Al. J. 24, April 24, 2020, https://ordentlichegerichtsbarkeit.hessen.de/pressemitteilungen/beginn-der-hauptverhandlung-gegen-taha-al-j.

40　Oberlandesgericht（Higher Regional Court）Frankfurt a. M., December 29, 2015, ECLI: DE: OLGHE: 2015: 1229. 4. 3STE4. 10. 4. 1. 15. 0A.

在叙利亚问题上，早在 2011 年，德国司法部门就已经启动了针对叙利亚冲突的结构性调查，所涉罪名包括战争罪与反人类罪。2017 年 6 月，德国联邦法院对叙利亚空军情报局局长贾米勒·哈桑（Jamil Al-Hassan）发出逮捕令，罪名包括杀人、酷刑、严重的身体和精神伤害以及非法拘禁等在内的反人类罪。[41] 德国科布伦茨高等区域法院分别在 2021 年 2 月 24 日和 2022 年 1 月 13 日判处一名叙利亚国民和一名前叙利亚情报官员犯有反人类罪与共谋反人类罪。[42] 此二人此前均已现身德国并已经在 2019 年被逮捕。[43] 因此，从立法和实践来看，德国的普遍管辖权应属于普遍关注加现身或普遍关注加条约、现身型。

## （四）法国

法国的普遍管辖权的立法主要体现在以下三部法律：《刑事诉讼法》《95-1 号法案》《96-432 号法案》。《刑事诉讼法》第 689 条第 1 款明确规定：根据下列条款所述的国际公约，任何在法国境外犯下这些条款所列任何罪行的人，如果在法国，可由法国法院起诉和审判[44]。随后，本条第 2 款至第 14 款详细列举了可依据的公约及

---

41　Bundesgerichtshof (BGH) (Federal Court of Justice), Investigating Judge, arrest warrant of June 6, 2018, 4 BGs 106/18, 3 BJs 18/18-4.

42　《秘书长关于普遍管辖权原则范围和适用的报告》（第 76 届联合国大会），A/76/203，2021 年 7 月 21 日，第 6 页。

43　Anwar Raslan and Eyad Al Gharib, accessed June 8, 2023, https://trialinternational. org/latest-post/anwar-raslan-and-eyad-al-gharib/.

44　*Code de procédure pénale*, Art. 689 (1).

如何适用这些公约。这些公约共 12 项，包括《禁止酷刑和其他残忍、不人道或有辱人格的待遇或处罚公约》（以下简称《禁止酷刑公约》）、《欧洲制止恐怖主义公约》和《国际刑事法院罗马规约》（以下简称《罗马规约》）等国际公约或区域性公约。[45]《95-1 号法案》和《96-432 号法案》分别是为了使法国法院得以管辖被前南刑庭和卢旺达刑庭判有罪的被告，依据第 827 号和第 955 号安理会决议制定。法国在提交给秘书长的材料中也指出"两项安理会决议使得法国法院（依据此法）的普遍管辖权受到属人原则、属时原则和属地原则的限制"。[46]

司法实践方面，在 2005 年 7 月 1 日的裁决中，加尔（Gard）省巡回法院判处一名毛里塔尼亚公民 10 年监禁，并为每名受害者支付 15 000 欧元的赔偿金和利息，罪名是 1990—1991 年在毛里塔尼亚实施的酷刑行为。这是法国首次此类定罪。2008 年 12 月 15 日的一项裁决中，下莱茵巡回法院裁定一名突尼斯公民哈立德在 1996 年 10 月担任警察局长期间，在突尼斯的警察局下令对一名突尼斯妇女实施酷刑，判处他八年监禁。[47] 上述两个案例均是基于《刑事诉讼法》第 689 条作出的，两名被告均具备"现身法国"这一要素。综上可见，法国承认的普遍管辖权是典型的普遍关注加条约、现身型管辖权。

---

45　*Code de procédure pénale*, Arts. 689（2）– 689（14）.

46　Permanent Mission of France to the United Nations, Ref: AT/sec No. 214, April 27, 2010, p. 4.

47　Ibid., p. 5.

## （五）英国

因为英国特殊的国内行政区划，英格兰与威尔士、苏格兰和北爱尔兰三个行政区域的普遍管辖权实践可能有所不同。整体而言，根据英国政府发布的文件，英国政府授权法院基于国际习惯法和各种条约规定的英国的国际义务，对于在某些令人发指的犯罪案件中适用普遍管辖权。[48] 可以认为英国行使普遍管辖权的类型是普遍关注加条约、现身型普遍管辖。

英国是《日内瓦公约》《罗马规约》《禁止酷刑公约》《防止及惩治灭绝种族罪公约》的缔约国。为履行条约义务，英国通过了《国际刑事法院规约法》（*International Criminal Court Act 2001*）、《日内瓦公约法》（*Geneva Conventions Act 1957*）、《灭绝种族法》（*Genocide Act 1969*）、《战争罪法》（*War Crimes Act 1991*）。但是在《国际刑事法院规约法》中，管辖权的范围限制在英格兰和威尔士地区内所犯下的灭绝种族罪、反人类罪和战争罪。[49]《日内瓦公约法》的第一条中规定：无论国籍、所在地是否在联合王国，只要实施、教唆、诱导他人作出违反本法的行为，都应当被认为犯下重罪并且应当被判处终身监禁或者不超过 14 年的有期徒刑；如果根据本条在联合王国境外犯下的罪行，可在联合王国任何地方对某人进行起诉、审判和惩

---

48　Government of the United Kingdom: Note on the Investigation and Prosecution of Crimes of Universal Jurisdiction, accessed June 16, 2023, https://assets. publishing. service. gov. uk/government/uploads/system/uploads/attachment_data/file/709126/universal-jurisdiction-note-web. pdf.

49　*International Criminal Court Act 2001*, accessed June 16, 2023, https://www. legislation. gov. uk/ukpga/2001/17/section/52.

罚，就如同该罪行是在该地方犯下的一样，该罪行应就其审判或惩罚所附带或随之而来的所有目的，均被视为在该地方进行；在苏格兰，四季法庭和治安官均无权审判本条规定的罪行，在英格兰，除非由检察长或其代表提起诉讼，否则不得提起此类罪行的诉讼，在北爱尔兰需要经北爱尔兰总检察长同意才可以审理此类案件。在英国发布的最新《关于调查和起诉可被普遍管辖罪行的说明》，对于酷刑和其他违反《日内瓦公约》的罪行的犯罪人，英格兰和威尔士地区的机构可以对现身于该地或者计划现身该地的人员启动调查和起诉程序，[50] 并且在实践中，具有普遍管辖权的罪行可以像任何其他罪行一样向警方报案。[51] 但是对于灭绝种族罪、战争罪和反人类罪，英格兰和威尔士法院只能对其国民或者居民行使管辖权。

皮诺切特引渡案在英国有关普遍管辖权的司法实践中较为重要。1998 年 10 月 16 日英国地方法院应西班牙法官的请求下令拘捕了正在伦敦就医的皮诺切特，他被指控涉嫌在任期内对西班牙公民及其后裔进行谋杀、施用酷刑和灭绝种族的罪行。地方法院的法官巴特尔特别裁定，西班牙法院有权根据调查皮诺切特在 1988 年之前的行为——包括建立秘密警察和针对皮诺切特在国外的反对者开展"秃鹰行动"，在 1988 年 12 月后继续进行并根据调查结果审判皮诺

---

50　Open Society Foundation, "Universal Jurisdiction Law and Practice in England and Wales," May 2022, accessed June 16, 2023, p. 1, https://www. justiceinitiative. org/uploads/33da3b6f-e6e6-4bef-8052-f87846113fe9/universal-jurisdiction-law-and-practice-england-and-wales-05232022. pdf.

51　Government of the United Kingdom, "Note on the Investigation and Prosecution of Crimes of Universal Jurisdiction," p. 3, accessed June 16, 2023, https://assets. publishing. service. gov. uk/government/uploads/system/uploads/attachment_data/file/709126/universal-jurisdiction-note-web. pdf.

切特。10 月 28 日，英国高等法院认为皮诺切特作为前国家元首享有免于英国民事和刑事诉讼程序的豁免权。随后这一决定又被英国上议院推翻，上议院在 1999 年 3 月 24 日的第二次决定中裁定，在 1988 年 12 月 8 日《禁止酷刑公约》在英国地方法院生效后，皮诺切特将军唯一可以被引渡的罪行是酷刑和共谋实施酷刑。法官以 6 票对 1 票的投票结果，认定皮诺切特因违反《禁止酷刑公约》的行为而不享有豁免权。最后英国内务大臣杰克·斯特劳（Jack Straw）鉴于 84 岁的皮诺切特糟糕的健康状况命令对其释放，从而使其回到了智利。

英国近年来涉及普遍管辖权的案件进入诉讼程序的较少，最近的案子主要是卢旺达政府自 2006 年起就开始向英国要求引渡在其境内犯下灭绝种族罪的人，但是英国在逮捕有关人员后，因为法院认为有关人员会受到不公正的审判违反《欧洲人权公约》第 6 条，因此拒绝引渡而将有关人员释放，目前卢旺达政府就此事还在积极与英国政府磋商。

综上所述，英国行使普遍管辖权的依据主要来自履行条约，并且在有关相关司法案例中也严格以条约为限，而在法律法规中也明确规定了不论犯罪人国籍和犯罪行为发生地但要求其身处英国，因此属于普遍关注加条约、现身型管辖权。

## （六）葡萄牙

葡萄牙的立场较为特殊，对灭绝种族罪、反人类罪、战争罪等罪行适用第三种普遍关注加条约、现身型管辖权，对计算机和通信欺诈罪、危害国家独立和领土完整罪、恐怖主义犯罪等其他罪行适用第一种纯粹的普遍关注型管辖权。由于缺少相应的司法实践，理论上葡萄牙可以被认为是以普遍关注加条约、现身型为主、兼有纯粹的普遍关注型管辖权的国家。

立法上，《葡萄牙刑法》第 4 条规定其空间效力通常及于葡萄牙境内和葡萄牙籍船只、飞机上。[52] 结合刑法第 5 条和葡萄牙根据联大决议提交的资料，葡萄牙刑法在以下情况可适用于境外犯罪：

（一）葡萄牙公民针对居住在葡萄牙的其他葡萄牙公民；

（二）葡萄牙公民或外国人对葡萄牙公民，如果罪犯是在葡萄牙境内被发现，且犯罪事实在发生地国应受惩罚，除非当地没有行使惩罚权，且无法进行引渡，或者由于欧洲逮捕令或对葡萄牙有约束力的其他国际协定而决定不移交罪犯；

（三）由外国人，不论受害者国籍，如果罪犯在葡萄牙境内被发现而无法进行引渡，或者如果由于欧洲逮捕令或对葡萄牙有约束力的其他国际协定而决定不自首；

（四）任何人，实施的"计算机和通信欺诈"罪，[53]

---

52　*Código Penal de 1982*, Portugal, December 21, 2021, Art. 4, last accessed June 8, 2023, https://www.codigopenal.pt/. ("Código Penal")

53　*Código Penal*, Art. 221.

"伪造货币、信用证书和封存价值物"和"伪造模具、重量和等价物"类犯罪,[54]"危害国家独立和领土完整"类犯罪,[55]"违反法治进程"和"违反选举"类犯罪,[56]恐怖主义犯罪,[57]以及恐怖组织犯下的特定罪行。[58]

上述第一点为积极的属人管辖权,第二点为消极的属人管辖权,第三点理论上体现葡萄牙的普遍关注加现身或普遍关注加条约、现身型管辖权。值得注意的是,在提交给联大资料的说明中,葡萄牙指出,上述第四点所列罪行是"涉及葡萄牙法律确立的绝对的普遍管辖权的罪行"(absolute universal jurisdiction),[59]因此应认为,葡萄牙在目前立法中保留了第一种纯粹的普遍关注型管辖权的存在。

同时,葡萄牙于 2002 年加入国际刑事法院,并在 2004 年 7 月通过《使葡萄牙刑事立法适应〈国际刑事法院规约〉的第 31/2004

---

54　*Código Penal*, Arts. 262–271.

55　Ibid. , Arts. 308–321.

56　Ibid. , Arts. 325–345.

57　*Law 52/2003 of August 2003 on Combating Terrorism, Portugal*, amended in 2015, Art. 2, accessed January 1, 2023, https://gddc. ministeriopublico. pt/sites/default/files/documentos/pdf/52-2003_terrorismo_ revistamarco21. pdf (*Law 52/2003*).

58　*Law 52/2003*, Art. 4; See also in *Código Penal*, Art. 5 ( 1 ); See also "Information provided by Portugal on the scope of universal jurisdiction in accordance with General Assembly resolution 64/117", Portugal, in UNGA, Sixth Committee, Sixty-fifth session, October 4, 2010, pp. 1–2, last accessed June 8, 2023, https://www. un. org/en/ga/sixth/65/ScopeAppUniJuri_ StatesComments/Portugal. pdf ("Information provided by Portugal").

59　Information provided by Portugal, p. 2.

号法律》。[60] 根据该法律，《葡萄牙刑法》增加了《与违反国际人道法行为有关的刑法》附件，附件第 5 条规定，"附件管辖罪行也适用于在葡萄牙境外实施的行为，如果行为人在葡萄牙境内且无法引渡，或已决定不将行为人移交国际刑事法院"。[61] 而该附件包括灭绝种族罪[62]、反人类罪[63]、战争罪[64]、煽动战争和招募雇佣军在内的[65]四类违反国际人道法的犯罪在《葡萄牙刑法》中的规定，并于第 2 条定义部分指明《日内瓦公约》及其附件议定书、《消除一切形式种族歧视公约》《消除对妇女一切形式歧视公约》《儿童权利公约》等法律渊源。[66] 在提交给联大资料的说明中，葡萄牙也指出，"葡萄牙法律（对这些罪行）规定了有条件的普遍管辖权"（conditional universal jurisdiction）。[67] 据此，应认为对于上述四罪，葡萄牙采取了普遍关注加条约、现身型管辖权。

综上所述，葡萄牙对违反国际人道法四罪采用普遍关注加条约、现身型管辖权，对于违反欧盟法、国内法和有关恐怖主义犯罪

60　Law No. 31/2004 adapting Portuguese criminal legislation to the Statute of the International Criminal Court, Portugal, July 22, 2004, accessed accessed on June 8, 2023, https://www.derechos.org/intlaw/doc/prticc2.html.

61　Criminal law pertaining to violations of international humanitarian law, Annex of *Código Penal*, 2004, Art. 5（1）, last accessed June 8, 2023, https://www.derechos.org/intlaw/doc/prticc2.html（*"Criminal law pertaining to violations of international humanitarian law"*）.

62　Criminal law pertaining to violations of international humanitarian law, Art. 8.

63　Ibid., Art. 9.

64　Ibid., Arts. 10-16.

65　Ibid., Arts. 17-18.

66　Ibid., Art. 2.

67　Information provided by Portugal, p. 2.

等六罪采用纯粹的普遍关注型管辖权。考虑到罪行性质的严重程度和立法的普遍性，应认为葡萄牙目前是以普遍关注加条约、现身型为主、兼有纯粹的普遍关注型管辖权的国家。

## （七）俄罗斯

俄罗斯的普遍管辖权更接近普遍关注加条约、现身型管辖权。《俄罗斯联邦刑法典》设专章规定了危害人类和平与安全罪，认为四类行为构成本章规定之罪行：计划、准备、发起侵略战争（第353条）；公开呼吁发动侵略战争（第354条）；使用被禁止的作战手段（第356条）；灭绝种族（第357条）。[68] 同时，根据该法第12条，在俄罗斯联邦境外犯罪的外国国民和无国籍人，在违反了俄罗斯联邦参加的国际协定的情况下，也应根据本法承担刑事责任。[69]《俄罗斯联邦宪法》也规定"公认的国际法原则和规范以及俄罗斯联邦参加的国际条约应成为其法律制度的组成部分。如果俄罗斯联邦的国际条约规定了法律规定以外的规则，则应适用国际条约的规则"，[70] 确认了俄罗斯加入的国际条约在其国内法体系中的地位。2003年，俄罗斯联邦最高法院在《关于普通管辖权法院适用普遍公认的国际法原则和规范以及俄罗斯联邦国际条约的裁决》中，进一步对俄罗斯法院适用国际条约的问题作出了说明。其中指出，如果

---

68　*The Criminal Code of the Russian Federation*, No. 63-FZ of June 13, 1996, Art. 353, Art. 354, Art. 356, Art. 358.

69　Ibid., Art. 12 (3).

70　*The Constitution of Russian Federation*, December 1, 1993, Art. 15 (4).

俄罗斯加入的条约本身不要求缔约国以颁布法律的形式履行条约，则在审议民事、刑事或行政案件时，法院应直接适用这些条约。但同时，包括国家元首、政府首脑、外交使团团长、成员及家属在内的外国外交代表或其他公民在俄境内享有豁免权。[71] 此裁决特别强调了在《欧洲人权公约》框架下，俄罗斯接受欧洲人权法院对《欧洲人权公约》解释和适用的强制管辖权。[72] 但是，在 2022 年乌克兰危机爆发后，俄罗斯于当年 3 月 15 日宣布退出欧洲委员会，《欧洲人权公约》也不再对俄生效。[73] 在 2023 年的一次会议上，俄罗斯总统普京再次指出，欧洲人权法院的一些裁决变得"公开政治化"，具有"偏见和偏袒"，因此俄罗斯退出其管辖范围。[74]

实践中，俄罗斯对普遍管辖权的态度比较谨慎。在俄罗斯提交给联大第六委员会的声明中，俄罗斯代表认为应当"极其审慎"地

71　See generally in Supreme Court Ruling on Application of Universally Recognized Principles and Norms of International Law and of International Treaties of the Russian Federation by Courts of General Jurisdiction, October 10, 2003. 俄罗斯的普通管辖权法院包括：俄罗斯联邦最高法院、共和国、边疆区、州最高法院，联邦直辖市法院，自治州法院，自治区法院，区域法院，军事法院和专业法院，参见 Law on Courts of General Jurisdiction, February 7, 2011, Art. 1。

72　Supreme Court Ruling on Application of Universally Recognized Principles and Norms of International Law and of International Treaties of the Russian Federation by Courts of General Jurisdiction, October 10, 2003.

73　Foreign Ministry statement on initiating the process of withdrawing from the Council of Europe, March 15, 2022, accessed July 29, 2023, https://mid.ru/en/foreign_policy/news/1804379/.

74　Meeting of judges of general jurisdiction, military and arbitration courts, February 14, 2023, accessed July 29, 2023, http://en.kremlin.ru/events/president/news/70510.

对待普遍管辖权的使用，尤其要尊重官方人士的豁免权。[75] 在兰采夫诉塞浦路斯和俄罗斯 （*Case of Rantsev v Cyprus and Russia*） 一案中，原告兰采夫是俄罗斯公民，其女儿在塞浦路斯身故，他遂起诉俄罗斯政府违反《欧洲人权公约》第 2 条和第 4 条，认为俄政府没有对其女儿被贩卖和死亡进行充分调查，也没有采取有效措施保护其女免受贩卖。[76] 本案中，俄罗斯认为事件发生在其领土之外，尽管俄罗斯负有保护人权的条约义务，但它在塞浦路斯共和国领土没有 "实际权力" （actual authority），俄罗斯的行为将受塞浦路斯共和国主权的限制。[77] 这表明，俄罗斯认为即便在有条约义务的情况下，国家域外管辖权的行使也应让位于他国主权。作为处理严重国际罪行的主要司法机构，国际刑事法院第二预审分庭于 2023 年 3 月 17 日向俄罗斯总统普京和总统办公室儿童权利专员利沃瓦－贝洛娃发出逮捕令，[78] 俄罗斯外交部随即作出回应，称 "俄罗斯没有也不会与国际刑事法院合作，从法律角度来看，它对我国公民没有管辖

---

[75] Statement by Representative of the Russian Federation in the Sixth Committee of the 68th Session of the General Assembly on Agenda Item, "The Scope and Application of the Principle of Universal Jurisdiction", October 17, 2013, accessed July 30, 2023, https://www.un.org/en/ga/sixth/68/pdfs/statements/universal_jurisdiction/russia_e.pdf.

[76] *Case of Rantsev v Cyprus and Russia*, Application no. 25965/04, Judgment, January 7, 2010, para. 3.

[77] Ibid., para. 203. 事实上，即便是欧洲人权法院也认为，《欧洲人权公约》第 2 条所规定的生命权受侵害事件得到有效调查的义务并不意味着成员国必须在刑法中规定对涉及本国国民死亡的案件拥有普遍管辖权，见本案判决第 244 段。

[78] Situation in Ukraine: ICC judges issue arrest warrants against Vladimir Vladimirovich Putin and Maria Alekseyevna Lvova-Belova, March 17, 2023, accessed May 6, 2024, https://www.icc-cpi.int/news/situation-ukraine-icc-judges-issue-arrest-warrants-against-vladimir-vladimirovich-putin-and.

权，其行动是无效的"。[79] 这表明俄罗斯对待普遍管辖权的态度正在趋于强硬，因为它可能被用于进一步攻击俄罗斯领导人。

# 二、亚洲

亚洲地区幅员辽阔，涉及大陆、海洋、伊斯兰等多种法系的国家。由于意识形态、法律文化、宗教信仰等原因，亚洲国家没有形成统一的司法趋势。因此，本章以地理区域进行区分，分析东亚、南亚及东南亚地区、中亚及西亚地区三个区域中各国的普遍管辖权实践。

## （一）东亚地区

### 韩国

韩国的国家实践属于普遍关注加条约、现身型管辖权。

韩国根据《大韩民国宪法》第 6 条第 1 款："正式缔结和颁布的条约和公认的国际法规则应与大韩民国的国内法具有同等效力。"韩国于 2002 年 11 月 13 日批准了《罗马规约》并于 2007 年 12 月 21 日出台了 8719 号《惩治国际刑事法院管辖范围内的犯罪行为法》，在第 3 条中对适用问题进行规定："（5）本法适用于在大韩民国境

---

79　Briefing by Foreign Ministry Spokeswoman Maria Zakharova, March 30, 2023, accessed July 29, 2023, https://mid. ru/en/foreign_policy/news/1860654/#34.

外犯下灭绝种族等罪行并在大韩民国境内停留的任何外国人。"

另外，在一些特别法中，也可见诸如此类的表述，如《关于防止非法贩运麻醉品的特殊案件法》第 12 条（海外犯罪）："第 6 条至第 8 条和第 10 条中的罪行应适用于按照《刑法》第 5 条的例子在韩国境外犯下此类罪行的外国人。"

《破坏船舶和海上结构的惩罚法》第 3 条（对外国人的适用范围）："本法也应适用于属于以下任何一项的外国人……3. 在大韩民国境外犯下第 5 条至第 13 条任何规定的罪行并在大韩民国境内逗留的外国人。"

《防止为威胁公众而购买金钱法》第 3 条（外汇和对外国人的适用）："本法也适用于属于以下任何一项的外国人……3. 在大韩民国境外犯下第 6 款规定的罪行并在大韩民国境内停留的外国人。"

由此可见，"在韩国境内停留或逗留"成为韩国行使管辖权的一个重要连接点。

1983 年卓长仁劫机案是韩国行使普遍管辖权的一次司法实践。1983 年 5 月 5 日，中国人卓长仁协同 5 人劫持一架中国民航客机降落在韩国春川机场，后被韩国警方逮捕。韩国最高法院裁定，虽然管辖权主要属于飞机注册国，即中国，但考虑到 1970 年缔结的《关于制止非法劫持航空器的公约》第 1、第 3、第 4 和第 7 条，韩国也可以要求同时拥有管辖权，因为被劫持的飞机降落在其境内。因此依据韩国国内《航空器航行安全法》，被认为适用于在国外犯罪的外国劫持者。

本案中，劫机行为发生在韩国领土之外，不涉及韩国的罪犯或受害者，被劫持的飞机仅仅恰好降落在其领土上。辩护律师认为，韩国司法机构对此案没有管辖权，因为该罪行没有援引《大韩民国刑法》规定的任何管辖权原则，如属地性、国籍或特别保护的利益。然而，法院坚持认为，韩国确实可以根据《关于制止非法劫持航空器的公约》行使管辖权，并监禁了劫机者。[80] 尽管法院的裁决没有明确提到普遍管辖权，但很明显，这是导致法院在此案中主张管辖权的指导原则。

## （二）南亚及东南亚地区

针对南亚及东南亚地区，本文主要考察了印度、斯里兰卡、新加坡、越南、孟加拉国五个国家。就结论而言，其中大部分国家都是普遍关注加条约、现身型管辖权。

### 1. 印度

印度关于普遍管辖权的立法主要是 1960 年颁布的《日内瓦公约法》。该法序言明确写明其是为了在印度境内实施《日内瓦公约》。[81] 第 3 条规定，任何人，不论其国籍，如果在印度境内外实

---

80　Information provided by the Republic of Korea on the scope of universal jurisdiction in accordance with General Assembly resolution 64/117. The scope and application of the principle of universal jurisdiction (Agenda item 86), General Assembly of the United Nations, Sixth Committee (Legal), sixty-fifth session, October 4 to November 11, 2010.

81　The Gazette of India, Extraordinary, Part Ⅱ-Section 1, No. 7, New Delhi, March 12, 1960, p. 51. *The Geneva Conventions Act 1960*, Art. 1.

施、企图实施或教唆他人实施严重违反《日内瓦第一公约》第50条、《日内瓦第二公约》第51条、《日内瓦第三公约》第130条和《日内瓦第四公约》第147条的行为，将受到处罚。[82] 该法第4条紧接着就"任何人实施于印度领土之外的、违反本法的行为"作了规定，并且指出"可将其视为在印度境内的任何地方犯下的罪行进行处理"。[83] 虽然第3条、第4条似乎赋予了印度国内法院管辖外国人的权力，但其第1条第2款却将这种权力明确限制在"印度境内"，[84] 这意味着即便外国人在印度境外实施了相关罪行，也只有在进入印度境内后，才能受到该法规制。又因为该法实际上是对《日内瓦公约》的转化，具体而言，是对其第49条的义务履行。可见，印度对相关罪行行使的普遍管辖权是普遍关注加条约、现身型管辖权。此外，根据印度外交部在答复为何不加入《罗马规约》时的答复，[85] 以及印度与美国之间有关不引渡对方公民给国际法庭的协定，[86] 似乎都表明印度政府对于由国际组织在更广的范围内行使普遍管辖权十分谨慎。

---

82　*The Geneva Conventions Act 1960*, Art. 3.

83　Ibid. , Art. 4.

84　The Gazette of India, Extraordinary, Part Ⅱ-Section 1, No. 7, New Delhi, March 12, 1960, p. 51. The Geneva Conventions Act 1960, Art. 1 and Art. 2.

85　答复中，印度外交部如此回应：《规约》中存在若干缺陷……包括它将一些受国家管辖的罪行纳入法院的管辖范围，并且使国家管辖权的首要地位受到法院的满意程度的限制。See generally in Rajya Sabha Unstarred Question No. 1740 to be answered on 17-3-2005, accessed June 8, 2023, https://www.mea.gov.in/rajya-sabha.htm? dtl/11103/q+1740+setting+up+of+international+criminal+court.

86　See generally in Immunity for the citizen, accessed June 8, 2023, https://www.mea.gov.in/articles-in-indian-media.htm? dtl/12816/immunity+for+the+citizen.

### 2. 斯里兰卡

斯里兰卡在 2006 年通过了《日内瓦公约法》，其中明确任何人，无论其是否为斯里兰卡公民，只要在斯里兰卡境内或境外实施、企图实施、协助、教唆、密谋或促使任何其他人实施严重违反《日内瓦公约》的行为，将被视为犯罪。[87] 斯里兰卡法院目前也没有对外国人或无国籍人在斯里兰卡领土外实施的相关罪行行使过管辖权。与印度类似，斯里兰卡法院可行使的普遍管辖权属于普遍关注加条约、现身型管辖权。

### 3. 新加坡

新加坡于 1973 年颁布了本国的《日内瓦公约法》，其中规定"任何人，无论其公民身份或国籍如何，无论在新加坡境内或境外，犯下、协助、教唆或促使任何其他人严重违反《日内瓦公约》的行为，均应构成本法规定的犯罪，一经定罪应承担责任"。同时，该法还明确如果在新加坡境外犯下本节规定的罪行，可在新加坡任何地方对该人提起诉讼、起诉、审判和处罚，如同该罪行发生在该地方一样。[88] 新加坡依据《日内瓦公约法》行使的普遍管辖权是普遍关注加条约、现身型管辖权。此外，《新加坡刑法》通过第 3 条和

---

87　*Gazette of the Democratic Socialist Republic of Sri Lanka, Supplement to Part* II, *Colombo*, March 3, 2006. *The Geneva Conventions Act*, No. 4 of 2006, Sec. 2.

88　*Government Gazette（Acts Supplement）*, No. 11, 3 April 1973, p. 151. *Geneva Conventions Act*, Art. 3.

第 130D、130E 条,[89] 将发生在新加坡境外的灭绝种族罪纳入本国法院管辖范围,但是由于新加坡是《防止及惩治灭绝种族罪公约》的缔约国,此条文实际上是对《防止及惩治灭绝种族罪公约》第 5 条和第 6 条的履行,故也可以视为普遍关注加条约、现身型管辖权。不过,新加坡目前没有依据《日内瓦公约法案》或《新加坡刑法》有关条款判决外国人或无国籍人犯有相关罪行。新加坡代表在联合国大会有关会议上的发言表明,其认为普遍管辖权不能脱离国家官员的外国刑事管辖豁免、国家主权和领土完整等原则。[90]

## 4. 越南

越南《刑法典》规定,任何外国人或外国法人在越南境内外犯下罪行,如果该罪行侵犯了越南公民的合法权益或越南社会主义共和国的利益,或侵犯了越南所加入的国际协定的利益,则应受到本法的刑事起诉。[91] 同时,该法第 422 条和第 423 条分别对反人类罪、灭绝种族罪、战争罪进行了规定。但是,越南立法同时规定,有外交豁免权的人犯罪,应按照国际协定和国际实践处理,在没有相关协定或实践的情况下,应以外交途径解决。[92] 越南代表在联大的发

---

89 *The Statutes of the Republic of Singapore, The Penal Code 1871*, Sec. 3, Sec. 130D and Sec. 130E. Revised Edition 2008, November 30, 2008. 其中,《新加坡刑法》第 3 条规定:任何在新加坡境外犯罪且依法应受审判的人,其在新加坡境外所犯的任何行为,应根据本法规定,以与新加坡境内所犯罪行相同的方式予以处理。第 130D 规定了五类构成灭绝种族罪的行为,第 130E 条规定了本罪的刑罚。

90 第六十八届联合国大会第六委员会第 13 次会议简要记录,第 47 段,A/C. 6/68/SR. 13。

91 The Criminal Code of Viet Nam, Art. 6 (2), Art. 422, Art. 423, Art. 424, Art. 425.

92 Ibid., Art. 5 (2).

言中指出：在犯罪人出现在越南境内以及在决定不将该人引渡至另
一国的情况下，越南可行使管辖权，即使该人既非越南国民，也未
在越南境内实施犯罪。[93] 此外，越南代表还建议将现身要素作为未
来普遍管辖权框架的组成部分。[94]

据此，越南可对"侵犯越南公民合法权益或越南利益"的行为
行使管辖权，这是一种保护性管辖权，因为它的依据明显不是相关
罪行的普遍关注程度，而仅仅是侵犯越南公民或越南国家的利益。
而针对"侵犯越南所加入的国际协定利益"的行为，则应属于普遍
关注加条约、现身型管辖权。

### 5. 孟加拉国

孟加拉国的普遍管辖权类似于纯粹的普遍关注型管辖权，其主
要体现在其 1973 年的《国际罪行法庭法案》中。该法第 3 条规定，
本法庭有权审判和惩罚在本法生效前、生效后，在孟加拉国境内犯
下本法规定之罪的任何个人或团体，而不论其国籍为何。[95] 可以被
该法庭管辖的犯罪主要是：灭绝种族罪、反人类罪、危害和平罪、
战争罪。该法确立的普遍管辖权虽然没有条约或现身因素，但它实
际上针对的是 1971 年孟加拉国独立战争中犯下战争罪、反人类罪等
罪行的孟加拉国人，性质上类似于一部特设国内法庭的规约，且孟
加拉国也从未依据此法审判过外国人。

---

93　《秘书长关于普遍管辖权原则的范围和适用的报告》，第 6 页，A/67/116。

94　同上。

95　The International Crimes（Tribunals）Act, 1973. Sec. 3.

## （三）中亚及西亚地区

### 1. 伊拉克

伊拉克的国家实践相比之下较为特殊，伊拉克以"全面管辖权"（comprehensive jurisdiction）的术语称呼普遍管辖权。同时其国家实践属于普遍关注加现身型管辖权。

伊拉克《刑法典》第 13 条明确规定，"除根据领土或具体管辖权适用伊拉克法律的情况外"，普遍管辖权适用于"在伊拉克境内"的任何人，无论其国籍如何，只要在国外犯下破坏或扰乱国际通信和运输工具的罪行，或贩运妇女、儿童、奴隶或毒品的罪行，或成为其从犯。普遍管辖权的范围只限于上述罪行，不包括任何其他罪行。同时，普遍管辖权的具体适用须经本国司法部长批准。

《伊拉克高等刑事法院法》第 1 条第 2 款规定了伊拉克高等刑事法院的管辖权："对被指控在 1968 年 7 月 17 日至 2003 年 5 月 1 日在伊拉克共和国或其他地方犯下本法第 11 条（灭绝种族罪）、第 12 条（反人类罪）、第 13 条（战争罪）和第 14 条（违反伊拉克法律）所列任何罪行的每个自然人，无论是伊拉克居民还是非伊拉克居民，包括以下罪行：灭绝种族罪；反人类罪；战争罪；以及违反本法第 14 条所列伊拉克法律的行为。"[96] 就本条而言，首先，其对伊拉克高等刑事法院的管辖权作出属时与属事上的限定，将时间限

---

[96] *Iraqi High Criminal Court Law*, October 18, 2005, Art. 1.

定为 1968—2003 年，将符合国际普遍关注的罪行划分为三大类别。其次，在属地要素上，其并未将管辖仅限与"伊拉克共和国"境内，而扩展到可能进行谋划、指挥、支持等行为的境外"其他地方"。最后，管辖权适用的人群被扩展到自然人。虽然本条中的普遍管辖权类似纯粹的普遍关注型管辖权，但从该法第 1 条、第 15 条规定来看，该法律主要针对的是伊拉克前政权统治下，在伊拉克境内外犯下上述罪行的人，并没有足够的普遍性。[97] 因而此法类似于以色列的《纳粹与勾结纳粹法》，在适用范围上具有较强的针对性，这削弱了"普遍关注"作为伊拉克法院管辖依据的纯粹性。实际上，该法庭所有被判有罪的被告均为伊拉克人。[98]

## 2. 伊朗

伊朗《刑法典》授权伊朗法院对根据国际条约应受惩罚的犯罪行为行使刑事管辖权，条件是嫌犯在伊朗境内。伊朗法院对国际罪行行使管辖权须视伊朗是否加入相关国际文书，以及被告是否在伊朗境内而定。[99] 这表明伊朗法律中的管辖权是典型的普遍关注加条约、现身型管辖权。

---

[97] 该法第 1 条明确规定法庭只能管辖在 1968 年 7 月 17 日至 2003 年 5 月 1 日（即伊拉克复兴党执政期间）实施的相关罪行。第 15 条排除了官方身份豁免，但同时法条重点提及了国家总统、革命指挥委员会成员、总理或内阁成员、复兴党领导成员等特定身份。

[98] Judicial Decisions, accessed June 8, 2023, https://www.derechos.org/intlaw/irq.html.

[99] 第 64 届联合国大会第六委员会第 13 次会议简要记录，第 2 段，A/C.6/64/SR.13。

### 3. 阿塞拜疆

《阿塞拜疆共和国刑法典》第 12 条第 3 款规定，阿塞拜疆公民、外国国民和无国籍人士，凡是犯有危害和平与人类罪、战争罪或贩运人口、酷刑等罪行，以及阿塞拜疆作为缔约国的国际协定所禁止的其他罪行的阿塞拜疆公民、外国国民和无国籍人士，无论在哪里犯罪，都将受到刑法的刑事起诉和惩罚。[100] 在阿塞拜疆立法当中并没有提及条约或现身要素，但是阿塞拜疆向联大提交的材料中却指出，"阿塞拜疆对普遍管辖权的尊重源自打击犯罪的国际法义务。阿塞拜疆加入了打击恐怖主义，灭绝种族等罪行的诸、多边条约"。[101] 此外，阿塞拜疆是许多打击国际犯罪或跨国犯罪重要国际公约的缔约国，根据《阿塞拜疆宪法》，这些公约自动成为国内法的一部分。[102] 这表明阿塞拜疆的普遍管辖权真正来源仍是条约体制，而并非纯粹的普遍关注型管辖权。同时，阿塞拜疆尚无行使普遍管辖权的记录。因此阿塞拜疆的普遍管辖权属于普遍关注加条约型管辖权。

### 4. 以色列

以色列的主要立法具有纯粹的普遍关注型管辖权的特征。该国

---

[100]  *Criminal Code of the Republic of Azerbaijan of 2000*, Art. 12. 3.

[101]  "Information submitted by the Republic of Azerbaijan on the scope of the principle of universal jurisdiction in accordance with General Assembly resolution 64/11," accessed December 26, 2022, https://www.derechos.org/intlaw/doc/azeuj.html.

[102]  第 65 届联合国大会第 10 次会议简要记录，第 17 段，A/C. 6/65/SR. 10。

有关普遍管辖权的主要立法是《纳粹与勾结纳粹（惩罚）法》《防止和惩治灭绝种族法》《以色列刑法典》。《纳粹与勾结纳粹（惩罚）法》第 1 条便明确指出：本法主要是适用于在纳粹政权下的敌国（enemy country，"敌国"是指纳粹德国及其他轴心国、任何部分或全部处于轴心国统治下的被占领土）犯下"反犹太人罪""反人类罪"和"战争罪"的任何人；第 9 条则规定：犯有本法规定的罪行的人，即使他已经在国外（包括国际法庭或仲裁庭）受审，都可以在以色列受到审判。[103]《防止和惩治灭绝种族法》则规定在以色列境外实施本法规定的犯罪行为的人，可在以色列受到起诉和惩罚，就像他在以色列实施该行为一样。[104]《以色列刑法典》则作出了更广泛的规定，根据该法，以色列法院有权对在以色列国外违反包括《纳粹与勾结纳粹（惩罚）法》和《防止和惩治灭绝种族法》在内的五项法律的人进行调查。[105]

《纳粹与勾结纳粹（惩罚）法》规定了在纳粹政权时期，在敌对国家（enemy country）实施屠杀犹太人，危害人类的行为；二战时期，在敌对国家实施战争罪的人根据本法可以被判处死刑。[106]

就司法判例而言，"艾希曼案"是以色列行使普遍管辖权的代表。在判决中，耶路撒冷地区法院认为本案中判决的罪名不仅在以色列国内法是违法的行为，在其他的国际法中也被认为是犯罪，判

---

[103] *Nazis and Nazi Collaborators（Punishment）Law*, Art. 1. and Art. 9.

[104] *The Crime of Genocide（Prevention and Punishment）Law*, Art. 5.

[105] *Penal Law of Israel*, Art. 4.

[106] *Nazis and Nazi Collaborators（Punishment）Law（1950）*, https://www.jewishvirtuallibrary.org/nazis-and-nazi-collaborators-punishment-law-1950, last accessed on June 16, Art. 1, accessed June 16, 2023.

决中列举了《防止和惩治灭绝种族法》、对德管制委员会 1945 年 12 月 20 日第 10 号法、纽伦堡审判判决的内容和对罪名的定义。列举的罪名包括反人类罪和战争罪，专有名词定义包括敌对组织（hostile organization），认为防止和惩治灭绝种族罪是国际社会众望所归，并确定了灭绝种族罪是国际法认可的罪名。[107] 关于管辖权问题，法院一方面认为自己依据《纳粹与勾结纳粹（惩罚）法》拥有对本案的管辖权；[108] 另一方面认为自己之所以可以依据以色列国内法行使管辖权，是因为《防止和惩治灭绝种族法》和《纳粹与勾结纳粹（惩罚）法》两部法律与《防止及惩治灭绝种族罪公约》和《国际军事法庭宪章》（《纽伦堡国际军事法庭宪章》）两项条约是一致的，而同时这两项法律也反映了习惯国际法，即灭绝种族是文明国家所公认的罪行。因而，实际上法院认为其管辖权来自条约义务和普遍管辖权两方面。[109]

### 5. 土耳其

土耳其的国家实践属于普遍关注加现身型管辖权。《土耳其刑法典》第 13 条规定："（1）土耳其法律应适用于在外国犯下的下列罪行，无论是否由土耳其公民或非公民犯下：a）第二卷第一章中定义的罪行（反人类罪、灭绝种族罪）；b）第二卷第四章第 3—8 部分

---

107　*Attorney General v Adolf Eichmann*, paras. 16-19, accessed June 16, 2023, https://www.asser.nl/upload/documents/DomCLIC/Docs/NLP/Israel/Eichmann_Judgement_11-12-1961.pdf.

108　Ibid. , para. 4.

109　*The Attorney-General of the Government of Israel v Eichmann*, Criminal Case No. 40/61, Judgment, paras. 16-19.

定义的罪行；c) 酷刑（第 94—95 条）……；d) 生产和交易麻醉品或精神药物（第 188 条）、为使用麻醉品或精神药物提供便利（第 190 条）；e) 伪造货币（第 197 条）；制造和交易用于制造货币和贵重印章的工具（第 200 条）；伪造印章（第 20 条）……；h) 扣押控制或劫持空中、海上或铁路运输车辆（第 223 条第 2 款和第 3 款）以及与损坏此类车辆有关的犯罪（第 152 条）。"此外，土耳其于 2003 年颁布了第 4912 号法律，目的是让土耳其法院对前南斯拉夫问题国际刑事法庭管辖范围内的罪行拥有管辖权。该法律要求被告人实际位于土耳其境内，同时优先考虑前南斯拉夫问题国际法庭的管辖权。[110] 需要指出的是，土耳其尚未行使过普遍管辖权。综上，对于前南刑庭管辖范围内的犯罪，土耳其行使的是普遍关注加现身型管辖权，而对于反人类罪、灭绝种族罪等罪行，土耳其行使的普遍管辖权更接近纯粹的普遍关注型管辖权。

# 三、大洋洲

本节针对大洋洲两个国家，澳大利亚和新西兰展开普遍管辖权的梳理与分析。

## （一）澳大利亚

按照类型细分，澳大利亚的实践应当属于第二类即普遍关注加

---

[110] 《秘书长关于普遍管辖权原则范围和适用的报告》（第 75 届联合国大会），A/75/151，第 47 段。

现身型管辖权。

目前，澳大利亚是《日内瓦公约》《罗马规约》《禁止酷刑公约》《防止及惩治灭绝种族罪公约》的缔约国，在其刑法和国会解释其行使普遍管辖权的文件中，明确规定其行使普遍管辖权的罪名包括灭绝种族罪、战争罪、反人类罪、酷刑，除了海盗罪和奴隶犯罪之外，其他的罪名都属于对条约义务的履行。

1995 年《澳大利亚刑法》第 268 条规定了禁止灭绝种族罪、反人类罪和战争罪。刑法第 274 条规定了禁止酷刑罪。所有这些罪行均适用于不受限制的 D 类管辖权，第 15 条第 4 款将其定义为管辖权的适用不受构成被指控罪行的行为或构成被指控罪行的行为的结果是否发生在澳大利亚影响，不要求受害者或肇事者必须是澳大利亚公民、居民或法人团体。[111] 并且，有关案件仅仅在被告出席的情况下进行。

为防止对第 268 条和 274 条下的罪行提起不适当的起诉，通常需要获得总检察长的同意才能开始起诉。虽然同意规则因犯罪类型而异，但对于完全在澳大利亚境外发生的犯罪，始终需要总检察长的同意。总检察长在行使酌处权决定是否应进行起诉时，可能会考虑国际法、惯例和国际礼让、案件是否正在或可能在外国被提起诉讼以及其他公共利益等因素。

对于海盗罪，澳大利亚仅仅对于发生公海即任何国家管辖范围

---

[111] Information submitted by Australia on the scope and application of the principle of universal jurisdiction in accordance with General Assembly resolution 64/117, accessed June 8, 2023, https://www.derechos.org/intlaw/doc/ausuj.html.

以外的地方或澳大利亚沿海地区进行的，且仅在肇事者或受害者的国籍、所涉船只的船旗国或与澳大利亚有任何联系的情况下适用管辖权。

综上所述，澳大利亚是上述规定受到普遍关注的罪行的公约的缔约国，同时也在刑法中规定了相应的条款以履行其条约义务。但是澳大利亚刑法对于其行使普遍管辖权的罪名范围并不限于条约规定，还包括了其他罪名，因此可以认为澳大利亚行使普遍管辖权的依据不仅限于条约。对于犯罪人的国籍和犯罪行为发生地都没有要求，因此并不属于体制内属地或属人的情形，并且澳大利亚对于有关案件不支持缺席审判，要求被告人必须现身于澳大利亚，因此澳大利亚行使的属于普遍关注加现身型管辖权。

## （二）新西兰

按照类型细分，新西兰应当属于行使普遍关注加条约、现身型普遍管辖权的国家。

新西兰是《罗马规约》《日内瓦公约》及相关议定书的缔约国。新西兰认为是如上的条约提供了其国内法中对于履行条约义务行使普遍管辖权的依据，[112] 并且新西兰行使普遍管辖权的罪名也都囊括在《国际罪行与国际刑事法院法案》（*International Crimes and International Criminal Court Act, 2000*）当中。根据本法第 8 条第 1 款的规定，不

---

[112] Information submitted by New Zealand on the scope and application of the principle of universal jurisdiction, accessed June 8, 2023, https://www.derechos.org/intlaw/doc/nzluj.html.

论被告人的国籍，犯罪行为是否发生在新西兰，或者被指控人在犯罪发生时或者决定指控该人犯罪时此人是否在新西兰都可以因为其触犯第 9 条（灭绝种族罪）、第 10 条（反人类罪）和第 11 条（战争罪）而提起诉讼。

本法第 13 条规定，未经总检察长同意，不得在任何新西兰法院对违反第 9 条、第 10 条和第 11 条的罪行提起诉讼。但这并不排除被控犯有上述罪行的人被逮捕或发出和执行逮捕令，也不排除被指控的人被还押或保释。

新西兰《日内瓦公约法》（*Geneva Convention Act*）也同样规定了未经总检察长许可，不得以违反第 3 条的罪名起诉任何人，在该法的规定中，不论当事人的国籍和公民身份为何，在新西兰或其他地方犯下、或帮助、教唆或促使他人犯下严重违反任何公约或第一议定书的行为，即构成可公诉罪行。[113]

在新西兰，几乎没有适用上述法规的案例，在 2006 年，新西兰曾经根据《国际罪行与国际刑事法院法》对前来访问的以色列将军摩西·亚阿隆（Moshe Ya'alon）提起诉讼，但是因为证据不足一直没能得到总检察长的许可，因此最终这一案件于 2006 年 11 月 28 日失效。在大赦国际的年度报告中也基本没有新西兰的案件信息。

综上所述，新西兰在提交给联合国大会的关于普遍管辖权原则的范围和适用的资料中明确提及其普遍管辖权的来源是条约，并且

---

113 The Government of New Zealand: Information submitted by New Zealand on the scope and application of the principle of universal jurisdiction, accessed June 16, 2023, https://www.derechos.org/intlaw/doc/nzluj.html.

要求犯罪人需要在新西兰现身，因此行使的是属于普遍关注加条约、现身型的管辖权。

## 四、美洲

北美地区的两个国家中，加拿大作为《罗马规约》的缔约国，以公约义务为框架搭建了其国内有关普遍管辖权的立法，对一切触犯了相关罪名的人，不论犯罪发生地或国籍国是否为加拿大，都将根据《危害人类与战争罪法案》（*Crimes Against Humanity and War Crimes Act, 2000*）对其行使管辖权。[114]而美国的立法与实践更具特殊性，因此在北美部分将以美国为重点进行分析。

另外，本文还选择阿根廷、巴西、智利、古巴、墨西哥五个具有代表性的拉丁美洲国家，就其普遍管辖权的类型和国家实践进行分析。拉美国家普遍管辖权多为普遍关注加条约、现身型管辖权，但也有国家（如阿根廷）为纯粹的普遍关注型，有些国家还有自身特殊的关切。

### （一）北美地区

#### 美国

美国适用普遍管辖权的类型应当属于普遍关注加现身型管

---

[114] *Canada Crimes Against Humanity and War Crimes Act*, last accessed May 8, 2024, https://laws-lois. justice. gc. ca/eng/acts/C-45. 9/page-1. html#h-114689.

辖权。

美国在刑事诉讼和民事诉讼中都涉及普遍管辖权的问题。其中，在刑事诉讼方面，因为不允许对刑事案件缺席审判，刑事普遍管辖权法规一般要求被告位于或在美国被发现。美国很早就建立了对海盗罪的普遍管辖，同样要求现身的因素，"任何人在公海犯下国际法所定义的海盗罪，随后被带入美国或在美国被发现，均应被终身监禁"。[115] 此外，美国还对奴隶制和奴隶贸易、种族灭绝、酷刑等实施普遍管辖。[116]

不过，对于一些得到较多共识的行使普遍管辖权的情形，美国并未全部纳入普遍管辖的范围，如反人类罪和战争罪。美国并未制定有关反人类罪的联邦立法，而美国的战争罪的被告范围仅限美国人或美国武装部队成员。[117]

另外，对于恐怖主义犯罪和麻醉品贸易犯罪是否适用普遍管辖权，联邦法院之间存在争议。比如在"美国诉尤瑟夫案"（*Case of United States v Yousef*）中，联邦第二巡回上诉法院的判决中称："恐怖主义不能提供普遍管辖的基础"。[118] 但是，在"美国诉尤尼斯案"（*Case of United States v Yunis*）中，华盛顿特区巡回上诉法院则表示："劫持飞行器很可能是国际法所明确谴责的少数几种犯罪之一，对

---

115　18 U.S.C. § 1651.

116　The American Law Institute, *Restatement of the Law Fourth, The Foreign Relations Law of the United States, Selected Topics in Treaties, Jurisdiction, and Sovereign Immunity* (St. Paul: American Law Institute Publishers, 2018), p. 162.

117　Ibid., p. 162.

118　*United States v Yousef*, 327 F. 3d 56, 107 (2d Cir. 2003).

该罪行国家可以实施普遍管辖权以审判犯罪嫌疑人，即使国家与劫机行为没有领土联系，且不涉及其公民。"[119]同样，联邦法院对于《海上禁毒执法法》是否创立了对海上麻醉品贸易的普遍管辖权存在争议。[120]

尽管对于民事诉讼中能否适用普遍管辖权或能否称之为普遍管辖权存在争议，但学者一般认为《外国人侵权法》和《酷刑受害者保护法》使联邦法院能够对于人权诉讼行使一定的民事方面的普遍管辖权。

《外国人侵权法》主要目的是保护人权，该法赋予联邦法院对酷刑、法外处决、强迫失踪、反人类罪、残忍、不人道或有辱人格的待遇、长期任意拘留、种族灭绝、战争罪、奴隶制、国家资助的性暴力和强奸为案由的民事侵权诉讼案件的管辖权。该法有关诉讼中的被告人国籍不限，但必须现身在美国，并且必须在侵犯人权的行动中以官方身份出现或者是依据法律要求行事。《酷刑受害者保护法》相比于外国人侵权法案中管辖的罪名较少，只包括酷刑和法外处决，并且只有自然人可以成为被告，而且要求原告已经穷尽侵权行为发生国的救济手段，而被告必须是在以官方身份行事或者具备这一外观。[121]

---

[119] *United States v Yunis*, 924 F. 2d 1086, 1092（D. C. Cir. 1991）.

[120] The American Law Institute, *Restatement of the Law Fourth, The Foreign Relations Law of the United States, Selected Topics in Treaties, Jurisdiction, and Sovereign Immunity*（St. Paul: American Law Institute Publishers, 2018）, pp. 161－162.

[121] Torture Victim Protection Act note of 1991, Sec. 2, accessed June 8, 2023, https://www.govinfo. gov/content/pkg/STATUTE-106/pdf/STATUTE-106-Pg73. pdf.

总体而言，美国在民事方面的普遍管辖权实践较为特殊，为跨国人权诉讼提供了机会。但应当注意的是，在美国，现任国家元首（总统、国王、总理）、外交部长或具有外交豁免权的官员一般不会在人权诉讼中承担责任。然而，一旦他们离任，无论是国家元首，还是其他官员，即使是因任职期间犯下的侵犯人权行为也可能成为人权民事诉讼的被告。此外，无论是刑事方面还是民事方面的普遍管辖权，美国的实践一般都要求被告必须出现在美国境内，因此可以认为美国行使的是普遍关注加现身型管辖权。

## （二）拉丁美洲地区

### 1. 阿根廷

阿根廷的立法和司法实践更为接近纯粹的普遍关注型管辖权，阿根廷不要求被告人"现身"阿根廷境内。但其立法中指出了条约要素，即相关罪行的范围以阿根廷加入相应的国际公约为限。

立法上，普遍管辖权原则的依据最早见于 1994 年《阿根廷宪法》。根据该法第 118 条，"所有非由众议院享有的弹劾权引起的普通刑事案件，陪审团一经设立，应由陪审团决定。审判应在犯罪发生的省份进行；但如果是在国境外违反国际公法的案件，应在国会以特别法确定的地点进行审判"。[122] 在提交给联大第六委员会第 73 届和第 77 届会议的答复中，阿根廷援引宪法第 118 条表明其接受普

---

[122] *Constitución de la Nación Argentina*, Ley N°: 24. 430, Argentina, 1994, Art. 118, accessed on June 8, 2023, http://servicios. infoleg. gob. ar/infolegInternet/anexos/0-4999/804/norma. htm.

遍管辖原则,[123] 并将该条作为对灭绝种族罪、反人类罪、战争罪、酷刑罪、强迫失踪罪等罪行适用普遍管辖的国内法律依据。[124]

在具体适用上,阿根廷较为独特,其普遍管辖权原则不以被告人"现身"阿根廷境内为必要条件,而强调该原则的附属性和补充性,即如果该罪行此前未被当局或国际法庭起诉,那么阿根廷便可以启动调查,从而行使普遍管辖权。因此,阿根廷理论上拥有相当广泛和宽松的普遍管辖权。证据如下。

首先,阿根廷国会于 2006 年 12 月通过《关于执行〈罗马规约〉的第 26.200 号法律》,该法作为宪法第 118 条后半句指称的"国会特别法",直接援引《罗马规约》规定了灭绝种族罪、反人类罪和战争罪,[125] 其第 3 条规定:

本法适用于:

(a) 在阿根廷共和国领土内或在其管辖范围内,或影响将发生于阿根廷的罪行;

(b) 阿根廷当局代理人或雇员履行职务期间在国外犯下的罪行;

---

123 《关于普遍管辖权原则的范围和适用秘书长的报告》,联合国大会第六委员会第 73 届会议,A/73/123,第 2 页(第 73 届联大会议报告);《关于普遍管辖权原则的范围和适用秘书长的报告》,联合国大会第六委员会第 77 届会议,A/77/186,第 2 页(第 77 届联大会议报告)。

124 第 77 届联大会议报告,第 18—26 页。

125 Ley 26. 200 de Implementación del Estatuto de Roma, Argentina, December 13, 2006, Arts. 8–10, http://www. derechos. org/nizkor/arg/doc/ley26200. html, last accessed on June 8, 2023 ("Ley 26. 200 de Implementación del Estatuto de Roma").

（c）阿根廷国民或居住在阿根廷的人在阿根廷领土以外所犯的罪行，但被告在国外未被宣告无罪，或在国外被定罪但未服刑；

（d）阿根廷共和国加入的国际公约规定的情形。[126]

根据该条（d）款，阿根廷可以依据其加入的国际公约之权利义务而行使普遍管辖权，并不局限于（a）款"属地"原则和"保护"原则、（b）款（c）款"属人"原则。

其次，根据联合国大会就"普遍管辖权原则的范围和适用"的秘书长报告，阿根廷数年来的发言均强调普遍管辖权的附属性和补充性，而未将被告人"现身"一国领土作为限制条件。2018 年，阿根廷报告说，阿根廷适用普遍管辖原则表现为"对于在阿根廷境外实施且国籍原则和保护原则均不适用的罪行，如果认为是国际法罪行，则启动调查"。对于行使普遍管辖权的条件，为"须确定该等罪行此前未被起诉或没有被起诉的可能"，[127] "换言之，仅当所涉行为不能或尚未在其他地方作出裁决时，才可行使普遍管辖权"。[128] 在 2022 年的发言中，阿根廷再次强调："阿根廷司法当局行使普遍管辖权，作为属地原则、主动和（或）被动属人原则和保护原则的补充和例外。在援引普遍管辖权和展开调查之前，司法当局首先要确保受影响国家没有正在进行的调查，国际刑事法院也没有在调查这

---

126　*Ley 26. 200 de Implementación del Estatuto de Roma*, Art. 3.

127　第 77 届联大会议报告，第 2 页。

128　同上，第 4 页。

些事件。"[129] "当国家不愿意或不能够行使管辖权时，其他国家可以通过行使普遍管辖权来填补这一空白。"[130]

因此，阿根廷将"尚未被当局和国际法庭起诉的国际罪行"作为其行使普遍管辖权原则的条件，不要求被告人"现身"要素，这种较为宽松的模式理论上更接近"纯粹的普遍关注"型管辖权。

由此导致在实践中，阿根廷的普遍管辖权实践较为积极，尤其近年来相当活跃。阿根廷于 2010 年适用普遍管辖权原则，审理了1939—1975 年弗朗西斯科·佛朗哥（Francisco Franco）统治期间西班牙人犯下的罪行，2014 年审理了以色列人在加沙地区犯下的反人类罪案件。[131] 2018 年 11 月，人权观察组织（Human Rights Watch）向阿根廷联邦法院起诉沙特阿拉伯王储穆罕默德·本·萨勒曼（Mohammed bin Salman），要求阿根廷适用《宪法》第 118 条的普遍管辖权原则，对其"在也门代理人战争中犯下的反人类罪"和"可能参与卡舒吉遇害案"展开调查。阿根廷联邦法官阿里尔·莱霍（Ariel Lejo）办公室要求阿根廷外交部从也门、土耳其和国际刑事法院收集相关指控的信息。[132] 2021 年 11 月，英国缅甸罗兴亚组织（BROUK）及六名女性受害者依据普遍管辖权原则向布宜诺斯艾利

---

129　第 77 届联大会议报告，第 6 页。

130　同上，第 11 页。

131　Argentine Court Hears Allegations of Genocide against Myanmar Leaders, June 7, 2023, accessed June 25, 2023, https://www.rfa.org/english/news/myanmar/rohingya-argentina-06072023162250.html.

132　人权观察：《继阿根廷后，将在其他国家继续起诉沙特王储》，半岛电视台，2018 年 11 月 29 日，https://chinese.aljazeera.net/news/2018/11/29/watch-will-pursue-binsalman-in-other-countries-after-argentina，访问日期：2023 年 6 月 25 日。

斯法院起诉，指控缅甸军方对罗兴亚人的"持续的灭绝种族"行为，并获得立案。[133] 2023 年 6 月 7 日，罗兴亚人首次在布宜诺斯艾利斯出庭。[134] 值得注意的是，2021 年 6 月，某些非政府组织依据阿根廷《宪法》普遍管辖权原则向阿根廷联邦刑事法院起诉，以所谓"灭绝种族罪"和"反人类罪"对中国官员发起指控。[135]

## 2. 巴西

根据分类，巴西对普遍管辖权的立场属于典型的普遍关注加条约、现身型管辖权。

《巴西刑法》第 7 条"域外管辖权"包含了有关普遍管辖权的规定：

> 下列犯罪尽管在国外犯下，但仍受巴西法律约束：
> 一、犯罪：（一）危害共和国总统的生命或自由；
> （二）针对联邦、联邦的区、州、自治市、市政府、上市公司、政府控制的公司、政府设立基金会的财产或公共信

---

[133] Historic Decision by Argentinian Courts to Take Up Genocide Case against Myanmar, November 28, 2021, laccessed June 25, 2023, https://www.brouk. org. uk/historic-decision-by-argentinian-courts-to-take-up-genocide-case-against-myanmar/.

[134] 《罗兴亚难民亲赴阿根廷法院亲身揭露军方暴行》，亚洲电视新闻，2023 年 6 月 8 日，https://atvnewsonline.com/asean/251750/，访问日期：2023 年 6 月 25 日。

[135] UHRP and WUC to Submit Universal Jurisdiction Complaint to the Criminal Courts of Argentina for Genocide & Crimes against Humanity against the Uyghur People, UHRP, December 14, 2021, accessed June 25, 2023, https://uhrp. org/statement/uhrp-and-wuc-to-submit-universal-jurisdiction-complaint-to-the-criminal-courts-of-argentina/.

仰；（三）为公共行政部门服务的人针对公共行政部门的犯罪；（四）灭绝种族，当行为人是巴西人或居住在巴西时。

二、犯罪：（一）根据条约或公约，巴西有义务管辖；（二）由巴西人实施；（三）在巴西的飞机或船舶上犯下的罪行，无论是商业或私人的，当其在外国领土上未受审判时。

在第一项情况下，行为人根据巴西法律受到惩罚，即使其在国外被宣告无罪或定罪；

在第二项情况下，适用巴西法律须满足：（1）行为人进入巴西领土；（2）该行为在行为地国也应受到惩罚；（3）犯罪属于巴西允许引渡的罪行；（4）行为人未在国外宣判无罪或服刑；（5）行为人在国外未被赦免，且提出追诉的时间不在按照最有利法律确定的法定时效期间之后。

巴西法律也适用于外国人在国外对巴西国民实施的犯罪，当满足：（1）没有引渡请求，或请求已被拒绝；（2）司法部长提出请求。[136]

根据巴西向联大第六委员会第 76 届和第 77 届会议提交的回复，第 7 条第 1 款第 1、第 2、第 3 项依据保护管辖原则，第 2 款第 2、

---

[136] *Código Penal*, Brazil, December 21, 2022, Art. 7, accessed June 8, 2023, https://www.planalto. gov. br/ccivil_03/decreto-lei/del2848. htm.

第 3 项分别依据属人管辖和属地管辖原则，"只有在特殊情况且在明确和客观的条件下"，普遍管辖权才可以适用,[137] 即第 1 款第 4 项和第 2 款第 1 项及后文指明的"根据条约或公约"和"进入巴西领土"的两要件。巴西坚持"普遍管辖应仅限于国际条约规定的最严重犯罪，只有相关条约的缔约国才能行使管辖权"，且"被控行为人应始终位于打算行使管辖权的国家境内"。[138] 据此可认为，巴西属于普遍关注加条约、现身型管辖权，条约罪行主要为灭绝种族罪和酷刑罪。[139]

司法实践中，虽然巴西法庭从未适用过普遍管辖权，但最高法院在 95.595/2018 号人身保护令案中确认，普遍管辖连同国籍原则和保护原则，是巴西行使域外管辖权的基础。[140] 在若干案件中，最高法院认为普遍管辖权在引渡程序中的重要性，以及"行为人位于巴西境内是行使普遍管辖原则的先决条件"。[141] 值得注意的是，巴西在提交美洲人权法院审理的"Herzog 案"中提出第 9455/1997 号法律规定了"减弱的普遍管辖权原则"（mitigated universal jurisdiction）。[142]

---

137 《关于普遍管辖权原则的范围和适用秘书长的报告》，联合国大会第六委员会第 76 届会议，A/76/203，（第 76 届联大会议报告）第 2 页。

138 同上，第 11 页。

139 同上，第 13—14 页。

140 Permanent Mission of Brazil to the United Nations, New York, Brazil, May 4, 2021, p. 2, accessed June 8, 2023, https://www.un.org/en/ga/sixth/76/universal_jurisdiction/brazil_e.pdf.

141 Permanent Mission of Brazil to the United Nations, pp. 2–3.

142 *Case of Herzog, et al. v Brazil, judgment*, IACHR, March 15, 2018, pp. 79–80, accessed June 8, 2023, https://www.corteidh.or.cr/docs/casos/articulos/seriec_353_ing.pdf.

### 3. 智利

智利倾向于普遍关注加条约、现身型管辖权，总体态度较为保守。

国内立法上，《智利刑法典》第 6 条规定了刑事管辖权的原则，即 "智利人或外国人在智利境外犯下的罪行和简单犯罪，除法律规定的情况外，在智利不受惩罚"。[143] 这一点在其《刑事诉讼法》第 1 条中体现为："智利法院有权审理智利和外国人在智利领土上犯下的罪行，除非特别法、智利加入的条约或国际公约或国际法一般原则另有规定。"[144]《法院组织法》第 6 条第 8 款也指明，"下列在智利境外犯下的罪行和简单犯罪受智利管辖：……（8）与其他国家缔结条约中所包含的罪行"。[145] 由此可见，智利对普遍管辖权中 "条约" 要素的重视。

2010 年，智利在向联大提交的资料中说明："智利法院尚未依据普遍管辖权原则对任何被控罪犯行使过管辖权。" 并提出："为适用普遍管辖权，一国确立管辖权和起诉个人的能力必须在国际法中

---

143　*Código Penal*, Chile, December 13, 2022, Art. 6, accessed June 8, 2023, https://www.bcn.cl/leychile/navegar? idNorma = 1984.

144　Codigo De Procedimiento Penal（Ley 1853）, Chile, June 27, 2012, Art. 1, accessed June 8, 2023, https://www.bcn.cl/leychile/navegar? idNorma = 22960.

145　*Codigo Organico De Tribunales*（Ley 7421）, Chile, December 30, 2022, Art. 6, accessed June 8, 2023, https://www.bcn.cl/leychile/navegar? idNorma = 25563.

有坚实的依据，通常为条约形式。"[146] 2021 年，智利再次强调，"普遍管辖权必须在一般国际法的背景下……仅适用于国际法规定的严重犯罪，特别是反人类罪、战争罪和灭绝种族罪"。[147] 事实上，根据 2009 年《将反人类罪、灭绝种族罪和战争罪纳入刑事犯罪的第 20357 号法律》，智利已完成对上述三罪行使普遍管辖权的国内立法。[148] 鉴于其"普遍管辖权是一个复杂敏感的议题，援引该权力的国家必须仔细思考并进行合理性论证，以保证普遍管辖权不会破坏国家间平等原则"的观点，[149] 智利总体上对普遍管辖权较为保守。

### 4. 古巴

古巴行使的是普遍关注加条约、现身型管辖权，但古巴对于普遍管辖权原则应当适用的罪行观点较为特别。

《古巴刑法》第 5 条第 3 款规定："《古巴刑法》适用于在外国犯罪的外国人和非古巴公民、不住在古巴的人，只要行为人目前在古巴而且未被引渡，不管他们住在作案的国家境内或任何其他国家境内，只要罪行在犯罪发生地也应受到惩罚。要是这项行为侵犯共和国的基本、政治或经济利益，或者反人类罪、人类尊严和集体健

---

146 Información remitida por Chile de conformidad con la resolución 64/117 de la Asamblea General sobre el alcance y la aplicación del principio de la jurisdicción universal, Chile, 2010, accessed June 8, 2023, http://www. derechos. org/nizkor/chile/doc/chluj. html.

147 第 76 届联大会议报告，第 11 页。

148 Tipifica Crímenes De Lesa Humanidad Y Genocidio Y Crímenes Y Delitos De Guerra（Ley 20357），Chile, November 22, 2016, accessed June 8, 2023, https://www. bcn. cl/leychile/navegar? idNorma = 1004297&idVersion = 2016-11-22&idParte = 8746450.

149 第 76 届联大会议报告，第 11 页。

康，或者根据国际条约应予起诉的犯罪，则当别论。"同时第 5 款说明："本条第 3 款情形，只有在司法部长提出请求时才能进行。"[150]

值得注意的是，2010—2016 年向联大第六委员会提交的材料中，古巴都坚持"普遍管辖权应仅限于反人类罪"的观点，[151] 因为"这类罪行的性质，全球正义的原则已然优先于属地或属人原则"。[152] 虽然《古巴刑法》总则部分"列出的各种条款都强调，对危害人类和人的尊严的一切行为，必须进行起诉或实施最严厉的刑罚"，但其中却没有载明对反人类罪具体规定的条款。"'反人类罪'一词的概念定义和需要保护的个人合法权利的存在可以从对这种行为定罪推断出来"，并以危害国家罪、危害和平和国际法罪等子罪名列举于《刑法》特别部分。[153]

据此，由于古巴《刑法》将"行为人在古巴"作为行使的必要前提条件，且坚持管辖罪名应限于反人类罪（包含古巴缔结的国际条约要求，即危害国际法罪），因此属于普遍关注加条约、现身型管辖权。

## 5. 墨西哥

墨西哥也属于较为典型的普遍关注加条约、现身型管辖权

---

[150] *Código Penal (Ley No. 62)*, Cuba, June 26, 1997, Art. 5, accessed June 8, 2023, https://www.rightofassembly. info/assets/downloads/Penal_ Code_ of_ Cuba. pdf.

[151] 第 66 届联大会议报告（补充），A/66/93/Add. 1，第 3 页；第 67 届联大会议报告，A/67/116，第 8 页；第 68 届会议，A/68/113，第 9 页；第 69 届会议，A/69/174，第 16 页；第 70 届联大会议报告，A/70/125，第 4 页。

[152] 第 70 届联大会议报告，第 4 页。

[153] 同上。

国家。

根据 2018 年向联大第六委员会第 73 届会议提交的报告，墨西哥法院仅在以下两种情况时行使普遍管辖权：第一，对墨西哥有约束力的条约规定了普遍管辖权；第二，对墨西哥有约束力的条约规定了或引渡或起诉（aut dedere aut judicare）的义务。[154] 第一种条约直接义务下，根据《墨西哥刑法典》第 4 条，适用普遍管辖权须满足：（1）被告在墨西哥；（2）被告在犯罪地国没有最终判刑；[155]（3）墨西哥和犯罪地国都将所犯罪行定为刑事犯罪。第二种条约间接义务下，根据《刑法典》第 2 条，须满足：（1）对墨西哥有约束力的条约规定或引渡或起诉义务；（2）满足《刑法典》第 4 条要求；（3）未将被告引渡到请求国。[156] 两种情况下，"义务来源条约"和"被告在境内"均是不可或缺的前提条件，因此墨西哥属于典型的"普遍关注加条约、现身"型管辖权。

# 五、非洲

根据 2009 年"非盟—欧盟普遍管辖权原则特设技术专家组"的调查报告，[157] 许多非盟国家通过专项立法或特设条款，规定普遍

---

154　第 73 届联大会议报告，第 5—6 页。

155　Federal Criminal Code, Mexico, 2000, Art. 4, accessed June 8, 2023, http://www.oas.org/juridico/spanish/mex_res13.pdf.

156　Ibid., Art. 2.

157　AU-EU technical ad hoc expert group on the principle of universal jurisdiction: Report, 8672/1/09 Rev 1, April 16, 2009, para. 16.

管辖权可适用于严重违反《日内瓦公约》的行为。这种立法来源于殖民时代的法律，即 1957 年《日内瓦公约法案》（英国）和 1959 年《日内瓦公约法》（《殖民领土法》）。这些国家包括坦桑尼亚、博茨瓦纳、肯尼亚、莱索托、马拉维、毛里求斯、纳米比亚、尼日利亚、塞舌尔、塞拉利昂、斯威士兰、坦桑尼亚、乌干达和津巴布韦。

另外，某些具有大陆法系传统的非洲国家已经批准了《日内瓦公约》，并在此基础上进行国内立法以接受普遍管辖权，包括阿尔及利亚、安哥拉、布基纳法索、布隆迪、喀麦隆、中非共和国、乍得、科摩罗、科特迪瓦、刚果（金）、刚果（布）、吉布提、埃及、厄立特里亚、加蓬、利比亚和突尼斯。

上述国家实践可被视为普遍关注加条约、现身并体制内属地或属人型管辖权的具体化。其普遍管辖权的创设来源于条约义务。如津巴布韦于 2001 年修订了辅助《日内瓦公约》国内实施的特别法《日内瓦公约法》，其第 3 条规定："严重违反日内瓦公约：（1）任何人，无论其国籍如何，如果在津巴布韦境内或境外严重违反下列公约或第一议定书的规定，即（a）附表一中所列的公约第 50 条；或（b）附表二所列的《公约》第 51 条；或（c）附表三所列的《公约》第 130 条；或（d）附表四所列的《公约》第 147 条；或（e）《第一议定书》第 11 条第 4 款或第 85 条第 2、第 3 或第 4 款；应属犯罪。"

值得注意的是，目前没有非洲国家有效地行使过普遍管辖权。

## （一）南非

南非的国家实践属于普遍关注加条约、现身型管辖权。

根据南非向联大提交的关于普遍管辖权的报告,[158] 1996 年《南非共和国宪法》第 231 (4) 条规定，"国际协定在被纳入国家立法时即成为共和国的法律"。因此，南非作为缔约国，将许多受到国际普遍关注的罪行通过立法纳入国内法体系以实现管辖权，如 1972 年，南非将《关于在航空器内的犯罪和犯有某些其他行为的公约》(1963 年)、《制止非法劫持航空器公约》（1970 年）、《关于制止危害民用航空安全的非法行为的公约》（1971 年）纳入《民用航空犯罪法》中，以及通过 1999 年《核能法》纳入《制止核恐怖主义行为国际公约》。

南非在 2002 年通过第 27 号法案《国际刑事法院罗马规约实施法》，将《罗马规约》规制的四大罪行纳入南非的管辖权体系。其第 4 条规定："（3）为确保南非法院对本章的管辖权，任何人在共和国 50 个省之外犯下第（1）款所述的罪行，在下列情况下被视为在共和国境内犯下该罪行……b) 该人不是南非公民，但通常居住在共和国境内；或 c) 该人在实施犯罪后，在共和国境内。"本条确立了"现身"——犯罪人要出现在南非国境内的要素，因此属于普遍关注加条约、现身型管辖权。

---

[158] Information provided by South Africa on the scope of universal jurisdiction in accordance with General Assembly resolution 64/117, 2010.

## （二）安哥拉

就法律文本而言，安哥拉的国家实践可被视作普遍关注加条约、现身型管辖权。安哥拉《刑法》第 5 条（安哥拉刑法适用于本国领土以外的事实）清晰地规定了"条约""现身"的要素：

1. 除非有相反的国际协议，安哥拉刑法适用于在安哥拉领土上发生的事实，如果：

（1）构成第 240 条至第 243 条、第 245 条至第 250 条、第 281 条、第 282 条、第 295 条至第 305 条、第 315 条至第 318 条和第 322 条规定的犯罪。

（2）构成第 362 条至第 368 条和第 370 条至第 375 条规定的犯罪，且该机构在安哥拉境内被查获，不可能被引渡的。

（3）对安哥拉人的犯罪行为，从该行为人在安哥拉常住并在此被发现开始。

只要犯罪人在安哥拉境内被发现且不能被引渡，安哥拉对在安哥拉境外实施的刑事犯罪，特别是构成第 362 至第 368 条和第 370 至第 375 条规定的犯罪，即反人类罪、灭绝种族罪和战争罪，具有管辖权。

### （三）布基纳法索

布基纳法索的国家实践属于普遍关注加条约、现身型管辖权。2009 年 12 月 3 日该国通过第 2009-52/AN 号法律，确定了布基纳法索法院执行《罗马规约》的权限和程序。在第 17—19 条中详细依照《罗马规约》分别规定了危害人类、灭绝种族、战争罪的具体要件，另外在第 15 条中规定了管辖权，规定如下："布基纳法索法院对本法中提到的罪行具有管辖权，无论这些罪行发生在哪里，也无论犯罪者或受害者的国籍如何，只要被起诉者在国家领土上，即受本国管辖。"

布基纳法索通过特别法律，在国内法层面明确《罗马规约》的适用细则，同时明确提及"被起诉者在国家领土上"的要件，属于普遍关注加条约、现身型管辖权。

### （四）喀麦隆

喀麦隆提交给联大的《关于普遍管辖权原则的范围和适用的资料》中提及，[159] 喀麦隆没有关于普遍管辖权的具体法律。仅仅对《刑法》第 8、第 10、第 11、第 132 条中的一些条款赋予喀麦隆对某些罪行的管辖权。

如《刑法》第 11 条规定："共和国的刑法应适用于海盗、人口

---

[159] Permanent Mission of the Republic of Cameroon to the United Nations, New York, April 30, 2010, No. 345/DCN.

贩运、奴隶贸易或毒品贩运，即使是在共和国领土之外实施的行为。然而，任何外国国民不得因在国外犯下本节所述罪行而在共和国境内受审，除非该外国国民是在共和国境内被捕且未被引渡，且起诉工作由检察院负责。"

又如《刑事诉讼法》第642条第2款："喀麦隆批准的国际公约所规定的具有普遍管辖权的罪行应被视为普通法罪行。"

以及第699条规定：

一项罪行应被视为在喀麦隆实施：

（1）罪行的一个组成部分在喀麦隆共和国境内实施。

（2）欺诈性地改变喀麦隆共和国印章或伪造喀麦隆法定货币的罪行。

（3）违反与麻醉药品、精神药物和前体有关的法律的罪行。

（4）违反有关有毒废物的法律的行为。

（5）违反与恐怖主义有关的法律。

要构成喀麦隆法院的管辖权，无疑需要两个要件：其一，所犯罪行是普遍关注且为喀麦隆所缔结的条约规制；其二，必须找到与喀麦隆属地或属人的连接点。因此，喀麦隆的国家实践近似于普遍关注加条约、现身型管辖权。

### （五）埃塞俄比亚

埃塞俄比亚的国家实践属于普遍关注加条约、现身型管辖权。埃塞俄比亚《刑法》第 17（1）条规定：

> 任何在埃塞俄比亚境外犯下如下罪行的人，（1）违反国际法或埃塞俄比亚法律规定的国际罪行，或埃塞俄比亚加入的国际条约或公约的罪行……应根据本法的规定和下文提到的一般条件，在埃塞俄比亚接受审判。除非在外国被起诉后已作出最终判决。

在实践中，埃塞俄比亚非常重视《刑法》（2004 年）第 19 条的辅助适用（subsidiary application）原则。第 19 条第 1 款规定，埃塞俄比亚刑法只有在以下情况下才能得到适用：（1）被诉行为根据埃塞俄比亚法律或行为实施地法律符合起诉条件；（2）该被告在埃塞俄比亚境内尚未被引渡，或因犯罪而被引渡到埃塞俄比亚境内；（3）该行为在犯罪国没有得到赦免，根据该国法律也不禁止起诉。[160]紧接着，第 2 款又指出，对于在埃塞俄比亚境外犯下的违反国际法或国际普遍秩序的罪行（第 17 条），以及其他在埃塞俄比亚境外犯下的罪行（第 18 条），可以不用满足第 1 款规定的第（1）和第（3）两项要件。据此，对于受到普遍关注的罪行，埃塞俄比亚行使

---

[160] *The Criminal Code of the Federal Democratic Republic of Ethiopia 2004*, Art. 19（1）.

普遍管辖权必须满足"现身于埃塞俄比亚境内"这一要素，即第 19 条第 1 款第（2）项要件必须得到满足。

2007 年 1 月 11 日，埃塞俄比亚联邦高级法院对前总统门格斯图·海尔·马里亚姆及其共同被告的案件作出判决，其被指控犯有灭绝种族和反人类罪。在《特别检察官针对门格斯图·海尔·马里亚姆上校等人案的被告律师提出的反对意见提交的答复》中提道："我国已于 1948 年 12 月 11 日签署并于 1949 年 7 月 1 日无保留地批准了《防止及惩治灭绝种族罪公约》，……犯有灭绝种族罪或第 3 条所列举的任何其他行为的人应受到惩罚，无论他们是对宪法负责的统治者、公职人员还是私人。"[161]

检察官的论述满足了"普遍关注"加"条约"的逻辑，综上，就埃塞俄比亚的立法与实践来看，其属于普遍关注加条约、现身型管辖权。

---

[161] Reply submitted by the Special Prosecutor in response to the objections filed by the counsels for the defendants in the case of Col. Mengistu Haile Mariam, et al., May 23, 1995, Arts. 7-9.

# 附件

# Universal Jurisdiction: Concept, Logic, and Reality [*]

## Sienho Yee

## I. The Concept and Logic of Universal Jurisdiction

1. The perceived abuse in recent years in the resort to universal jurisdiction, particularly over African officials, caused the Group of African States to request in February 2009 the inclusion of an additional item on the "Abuse of the principle of universal jurisdiction" in the agenda of the 63d session of the United Nations General Assembly (UNGA). The request was accepted and universal jurisdiction has been a subject of heated discussion in the UNGA since that time. Debates were conducted on this topic in autumn of 2009. The UNGA then asked governments to submit observations and information on State practice. Again debates were held on the topic in the autumn of 2010. Further information has been sought and further work has been scheduled for 2011. [1]

---

[*] First published in: *Chinese Journal of International Law* 10 (2011): 503. The preparation of this article forms part of the work of Research Project No. 08 & ZD055 of the China Social Sciences Foundation. The comments of William Schabas and the reviewers of the Chinese Journal of International Law on a draft are much appreciated. All opinions are personal. This article was completed on September 12, 2011. The websites cited were current as of this date unless otherwise noted. Thanks go to Oxford University Press for re-use.

[1] For the Request and the Explanatory memorandum, see A/63/237 (February 3, 2009) and annex ("African Union memo"). For summaries of development and documentation, see UN 6th Committee websites: http://www.un.org/en/ga/sixth/64/UnivJur.shtml; http://www.un.org/en/ga/sixth/65/Scope AppUniJuri.shtml.

2. The comments and statements made by governments show that there is great confusion on the concept, the scope and application of universal jurisdiction. In order for us to properly understand universal jurisdiction, it will be helpful for us to recap the understanding of jurisdiction in general. Usually jurisdiction has three dimensions: prescriptive, adjudicative, and enforcement. It is said that national criminal jurisdiction[2] is normally justified on several grounds: territoriality, nationality, passive personality or protection of national vital interests. Sometimes the effects of an act upon a State are also assimilated to some of these principles. Sometimes a treaty may be considered an independent justification for the assertion of jurisdiction; whether a treaty without incorporating the normal links such as territoriality is a sufficient justification is a controversial question. Each justification for jurisdiction may inform its exercise and thus leads to a different type of jurisdiction. The different justifications enumerated above thus give rise to different types of jurisdiction generally characterized as territorial, nationality, passive personality and protective jurisdiction.

3. Given these considerations and given the fact that there is no internationally codified definition of universal jurisdiction at present, many proposed definitions and commentaries seem to have defined universal jurisdiction by an "absence" of the normal jurisdictional links to the national legal system attempting to exercise jurisdiction. For example, the Institut de Droit International ( IDI) in its 2005 resolution on universal jurisdiction, paragraph 1, states:

---

[2]　This article deals only with universal criminal jurisdiction.

Universal jurisdiction in criminal matters, as an additional ground of jurisdiction, means the competence of a State to prosecute alleged offenders and to punish them if convicted, irrespective of the place of commission of the crime and regardless of any link of active or passive nationality, or other grounds of jurisdiction recognized by international law. [3]

In the view of the IDI Rapporteur of the project, "It was ( the) absence of link between the crime and the prosecuting State that captured the essence of universal jurisdiction." [4] Similarly, the AU-EU Expert Report on this topic states:

Universal criminal jurisdiction is the assertion by one state of its jurisdiction over crimes allegedly committed in the territory of another state by nationals of another state against nationals of another state where the crime alleged poses no direct threat to the vital interests of the state asserting jurisdiction. In other words, universal jurisdiction amounts to the claim by a state to prosecute crimes in circumstances where none of the traditional links of territoriality, nationality, passive personality or the protective principle exists at the time of the commission of the alleged offence. [5]

---

[3]  Institut de droit international ( IDI) , Resolution on universal criminal jurisdiction with regard to the crime of genocide, crimes against humanity and war crimes, adopted in Krakow, 2005 ( http: //www. idi-iil. org/idiF/resolutionsF/2005_kra_03_fr. pdf) , para. 1 ( hereinafter, "IDI Resolution") .

[4]  Christian Tomuschat, Rapporteur of the IDI Commission on Universal Criminal Jurisdiction, as quoted in IDI, 71 ( II ) *Annuaire de l'Institut de droit international* ( 2006): 257; see also ibid. , 261.

[5]  AU-EU Expert Report ( http: //ec. europa. eu/development/icenter/repository/troika_ua_ue_rapport_competence_universelle_EN. pdf) , para. 8.

4. Behind the "absence" façade, however, rests the basis for such an assertion of jurisdiction, normally formulated this way: The alleged crime is an attack on the fundamental values of the international community as a whole ( i. e. , a violation of *jus cogens* or a species of law that is very close to that genus, however, described, such as *erga omnes* obligations), so that the crime is a matter of universal concern, considered as such by the international community as a whole, and that every State in the world has an interest in prosecuting the perpetrator. [6] Another instrumental reasoning, which may apply with greater force to some situations than in others, is that the exercise of universal jurisdiction is *necessary* in order to ensure that certain crimes be punished. For example, piracy, normally committed on the high seas, may go unpunished if universal jurisdiction does not exist. As such, these crimes are also of universal concern, perhaps of a slightly different kind. So understood, it would seem better to characterize universal jurisdiction as "universal concern jurisdiction", [7] in some contrast to other forms of jurisdiction such as "territoriality jurisdiction" "nationality jurisdiction" and "national interests protection jurisdiction". These terms would make immediately apparent the

---

[6] See generally ALI, Restatement of the Law, Third, Foreign Relations Law of the United States ( ALI, Restatement Third) , § 404 and the associated comments and notes; IDI Resolution, n. 3 above; and the IDI deliberations, IDI, 71 ( II ) Annuaire, n. 4 above, pp. 199–284; International Association of Penal Law ( AIDP), XVIII Congress in 2009, Resolution on Universal Jurisdiction, http: //www. penal. org/? page = mainaidp&id_ rubrique = 24&id_ article = 95.

[7] See ALI, Restatement Third, § 404 ( "A state has jurisdiction to define and prescribe punishment for certain offenses recognized by the community of nations as of universal concern, such as piracy, slave trade, attacks on or hijacking of aircraft, genocide, war crimes, and perhaps certain acts of terrorism, even where none of the bases of jurisdiction indicated § 402 is present") .

justification behind each assertion of jurisdiction. A definition of universal jurisdiction or universal concern jurisdiction should be the exercise of national jurisdiction, based on universal concern, over crimes that attack the fundamental values of international society. [8]

5. The logic of universal concern jurisdiction is easy to understand. Universal concern as a motivating force for national action was propounded by the International Court of Justice in the celebrated *Barcelona Traction* case in 1970. [9] That case was about diplomatic protection, and the Court's celebrated dictum therefore cannot be claimed as direct precedent or immediate support for universal jurisdiction. [10] But that dictum on this point is unmistakably of general applicability and can be considered the elaboration of the *ultimate* rationale for universal jurisdiction. There the Court said:

33. When a State admits into its territory foreign investments or foreign nationals, whether natural or juristic persons, it is bound to extend to them the protection of the law and assumes obligations concerning the treatment to be afforded them. These obligations, however, are neither absolute nor unqualified. In particular, an essential distinction should be drawn between the obligations of a State towards the international community as a whole, and those arising vis-à-vis another State in the field of diplomatic protection. By their very nature the former are the concern of all States. In view of the

---

8　See ALI, Restatement Third, § 404.

9　Case concerning the Barcelona Traction, Light and Power Company, Limited, Second Phase, Judgment, *ICJ Reports 1970*, 3.

10　See Rosalyn Higgins, *Problems and Process: International Law and How We Use it* ( 1994) , 57–58.

importance of the rights involved, all States can be held to have a legal interest in their protection; they are obligations *erga omnes*.

34. Such obligations derive, for example, in contemporary international law, from the outlawing of acts of aggression, and of genocide, as also from the principles and rules concerning the basic rights of the human person, including protection from slavery and racial discrimination. Some of the corresponding rights of protection have entered into the body of general international law (*Reservations to the Convention on the Prevention and Punishment of the Crime of Genocide, Advisory Opinion, I. C. J. Reports 1951*, p. 23); others are conferred by international instruments of a universal or quasi-universal character.

6. Intended to implement this idea, [11] Article 48 ( "Invocation of responsibility by a State other than an injured State") of the International Law Commission's Articles on State Responsibility, adopted in 2001, states: "1. Any State other than an injured State is entitled to invoke the responsibility of another State in accordance with paragraph 2 if: ( _ ) ( a ) The obligation breached is owed to a group of States including that State, and is established for the protection of a collective interest of the group; or ( _ ) ( b ) The obligation breached is owed to the international community as a whole. " [12]

7. Thus, as a general proposition, there are certain matters in the world that are of universal concern, and this universal concern is sufficient to justify

---

[11]　ILC Draft Articles on State Responsibility, art. 48, commentary, para. ( 8 ) , in *ILC Report 2001*, A/56/10, 321.

[12]　*ILC Report 2001*, ibid. , 56.

certain action on the part of States. Applied to our inquiry in this article, this rationale alone, or this rationale plus another factor, potentially would justify a State's exercise of universal jurisdiction. However, universal jurisdiction is not a necessary corollary of universal concern, even when that concern assumes *jus cogens* proportions. [13] The sole fact of the violation of a rule that attains the *jus cogens* status does not give rise to the jurisdiction of the International Court of Justice or another international tribunal, as the Court ruled in *Democratic Republic of the Congo v Rwanda*; [14] nor do violations of *erga omnes* rights or obligations alone, as the Court has also ruled in *East Timor*. [15] Consent alone founds international jurisdiction or the jurisdiction of international courts and tribunals. Although the justification of the exercise of jurisdiction by a national legal order, our inquiry here, was not in issue in either case, the same conclusion may be drawn that the violation of a norm having *jus cogens* or *erga omnes* character does not in itself give rise to universal jurisdiction for the national legal systems. Whether the potential of universal concern in justifying the exercise of national jurisdiction has been realized, or the extent to which it has been, would depend on what crimes would be considered by States generally as crimes of universal concern and whether this universal concern has in fact been also considered by States as sufficient to justify an exercise of such jurisdiction. The answers to these questions will depend on

---

13　See Paolo Picone, "The Distinction between *Jus Cogens* and Obligations *Erga Omnes*," in Enzo Cannizzaro ( ed. ), *The Law of Treaties beyond the Vienna Convention* ( 2011 ), 411, 421 – 422; but see generally Alexander Orakhelashvili, Peremptory Norms in International Law ( 2006 ).

14　Armed Activities on the Territory of the Congo ( New Application: 2002) ( *Democratic Republic of the Congo v Rwanda*), *ICJ Reports 2006*, 31, para. 64.

15　East Timor ( *Portugal v Australia*), *ICJ Reports 1995*, 102, para. 29.

the reality of the international law formation process. This is an issue that needs to be assessed according to the normal sources of law exercise under article 38 of the Statute of the International Court of Justice ( ICJ). That exercise will be attempted in Part II of this article. For now, let us briefly consider some general issues that may frame such an evaluation and help us to understand what may have factored into that reality.

8. As the term "universal jurisdiction" has been used by various people to indicate various things in varying degrees of density or looseness, it will be helpful to offer some clarifications on the typology of situations that may constitute universal jurisdiction, properly so-called, or resemble it. To make things clear, the following characterizations, in the order of strength of "universalness", can be used:

(1)"Pure universal concern jurisdiction". This form of jurisdiction would be an assertion of jurisdiction based solely on the universal concern character of the crime, without more. This would be the "pure universal jurisdiction" or "true universal jurisdiction". If considered legitimate, this form of jurisdiction would entitle, as far as the jurisdictional requirement is concerned, the prosecuting State to the extradition of the suspect from a foreign State, if other conditions are met. [16] Sometimes "universal jurisdiction *in absentia*" is used to describe this type of jurisdiction but this term can be confused with "trial *in absentia*" and is not preferred here. Included in this form of jurisdiction are: 1) A State unilaterally asserts pure universal

---

[16]    Cf. AIDP, n. 6 above, para. II ( 3); but see 2005 IDI Resolution, n. 3 above, para. 3 ( b).

jurisdiction; and 2) Hypothetically a treaty allowing States parties to assert pure universal jurisdiction over nationals of non-parties for crimes occurring on territories of a third party. In the latter situation, the treaty regime as a whole does not have greater authority in relation to a third State than a particular State party to it, and the treaty granting jurisdiction to the parties to the regime does not add anything to our assessment.

(2)"Universal concern plus presence jurisdiction". This is illustrated by a State unilaterally asserts jurisdiction over a non-national who is present in that State for crimes of universal concern that have occurred in a foreign State. This is not universal jurisdiction properly so called, as the presence of suspect may justify this form of jurisdiction as "territorial", to some extent, or "nationality" when the presence of the suspect is prolonged so as to assimilate it to nationality. When the presence of the suspect is fleeting (such as a weekend visit) or brief (such as a medical visit), such an exercise of jurisdiction gives rise to different characterizations: some call it universal jurisdiction, while others claim that this is jurisdiction with some connection. If the absence of a link between the crime and the prosecuting State is the essence of universal jurisdiction, then a fleeting presence of the suspect in the prosecuting State may not disqualify the assertion of jurisdiction as that of universal jurisdiction. However, to the extent that the law about a State asserting jurisdiction based on brief presence is made clear, notice would have been given to any potential suspect. If he or she still comes to that State, voluntarily making that connection, such an exercise of jurisdiction can be considered "non-universal", definitely not "pure universal concern jurisdiction".

(3) "Universal concern plus treaty and presence jurisdiction". This

situation is similar to Situation 2, with the added obligation or right from a treaty to assert jurisdiction on that basis. An illustration would be a treaty allowing parties to exercise jurisdiction over a national of a third State, if present in the prosecuting State, for crimes of universal concern that have occurred in a third State.

( 4 ) " Universal concern plus treaty, presence and intra-regime territoriality or nationality jurisdiction". This is similar to and narrower than Situation 3, with the added requirement that the suspect or the crime must be related to a party to the treaty setting up the regime in terms of territoriality, nationality or victim nationality. An illustration of an intra-regime nationality link would be a treaty allowing party A to the treaty to prosecute suspect B, a national of party C to the treaty, who is present in A, for crimes of universal concern that have occurred in State D, a non-party to the treaty. An illustration of an intra-regime territoriality link would be a treaty allowing party A to the treaty to prosecute suspect B, a national of a third State ( non-party to the treaty), who is present on the territory of party A, for crimes allegedly took place on the territory of party C to the treaty.

Among these situations, only the first situation is pure or true universal jurisdiction. The second situation moves away from pure and true universal jurisdiction but is closer to it than the other situations. Situations 3 and 4 are not universal jurisdiction in the true sense. The role of universal concern in justifying the exercise of jurisdiction in Situations 2 to 4 is, strictly speaking, redundant. Indeed, if presence triggers a treaty based obligation to exercise jurisdiction, that jurisdiction can be, as described by the Joint Separate

Opinion of Judges Higgins, Kooijmans and Buergenthal in *Arrest Warrant*, [17]
"really an obligatory territorial jurisdiction over persons". If we were to call
these situations "universal jurisdiction", "universal jurisdiction" would be
purchased at the price of diluting and cheapening the concept; we would be
playing a game of words.

9. Secondly, various factors may inform the international law making
process relating to universal jurisdiction, and these result in the reality of the
extent of acceptance of it. First of all, universal jurisdiction can be
rationalized as a system jurisdiction, for the protection of the interests of the
international system including the protection of human rights and the fight
against impunity, while employing the national legal systems, *faute de mieux*,
to perform that task because of the lack of a central government in what we
often call the "international community". In a way, the national legal systems
can be considered to be in a situation of "dédoublement fonctionnel". [18] As a
result, States hoping to protect the interests of the international system and to
contribute to its maintenance and promotion should have incentives to promote
the establishment and the application of the principle of universal
jurisdiction. Furthermore, relating to this systemic consideration, universal
criminal jurisdiction would seem to be necessary to implement or enforce *jus
cogens*, another important systemic factor. Otherwise, that concept would be

---

17　Arrest Warrant, Joint Separate Opinion of Judges Higgins, Kooijmans and Buergenthal, *ICJ Reports
2002*, 74-75, para. 41.

18　A term from Georges Scelle. See Antonio Cassese, "Remarks on Scelle's Theory of 'Role Splitting'
(dédoublement fonctionnel) in International Law," *European Journal of International Law* (EJIL) 1
(1990): 210.

toothless. Those States that have recognized the idea of *jus cogens* probably may also have incentives to be friendly to the idea of universal jurisdiction.

10. On the other hand, the exercise of universal jurisdiction may infringe, or at least detract from, the principle of sovereignty and sovereign equality and is easily subjected to political abuse including discrimination as manifested in selective prosecution, thus destabilizing international relations. Because of this, this form of jurisdiction has been described as "dangerous" by none other than Henry Kissinger. [19] Of course, any exercise of universal jurisdiction will most likely favor the big and powerful States. [20] If as claimed by some States and Judge *ad hoc* van den Wyngaert in *Arrest Warrant*, the question is "about what international law requires or allows States to do as ' agents' of the international community when they are confronted with complaints of victims of" heinous crimes, [21] one may immediately question whether such agents should be self-appointed by a particular State itself. This concern assumes a greater proportion if the *Lotus* dictum is allowed to prevail. [22] Furthermore, the political nature of universal jurisdiction is on full display when the attempt to exercise universal jurisdiction by States may indeed be tradable, as in the case of Belgium which decided in 2003 to scuttle its strong universal jurisdiction authorization when threatened by the prospect

---

[19]  Henry Kissinger, "The Pitfalls of Universal Jurisdiction, " *Foreign Affairs*, July–August 2001.

[20]  As pointed out by Shahabuddeen, in IDI Annuaire, n. 4 above, p. 228.

[21]  Arrest Warrant, diss. op. , *ICJ Reports 2002*, p. 141, para. 5.

[22]  See Part Ⅲ below, paras. 44–49.

of the NATO Headquarters moving away. [23] Also, the attempt can be shamed away at least to some extent, as, on my view, in the case of Spain which in 2009 dismantled its own strong universal jurisdiction authorization when Judge Garzon began to dig into Spain's old dirty laundry resulting from the Spanish Civil War. [24]

11. Obviously a regime of universal jurisdiction would present severe challenges to national reconciliation efforts such as those made in post-apartheid South Africa or in some Latin American States. As stated by Kissinger[25]:

> It is an important principle that those who commit war crimes or systematically violate human rights should be held accountable. But the consolidation of law, domestic peace, and representative government in a

---

[23]  5 August 2003 Act on Grave Breaches of International Humanitarian Law. As reported by none other than the person who did the threatening, Donald Rumsfeld, Known and Unknown: A Memoir (2011), 596-598. Rumsfeld reported a "frank and full exchange" with Mr. Andre Flabaut, Belgium's minister of defense, in which Rumsfeld made clear that NATO could move its headquarters again as it did from France when the host became hostile and that the American support for the building of a new NATO headquarters "would evaporate instantly absent a prompt shift in the Belgium government's position". Ibid., 598. Rumsfeld seemed to relish this: "The difference in style between a Chicago-born American and member of the European diplomatic corps was on full display in that conversation. From his demeanor I could tell he fully understood my point. Within two months of that conversation, the Belgian government repealed their law." Ibid., 598.

[24]  See Jaclyn Belczyk, "Spain Parliament Passes Law Limiting Reach of Universal Jurisdiction Statute," October 16, 2009, http://jurist.law.pitt.edu/paperchase/2009/10/spain-parliament-passes-law-limiting.php; Daniel Woolls, Baltasar Garzon, "Spanish Super Judge, Suspended Over Alleged Abuse," AP News (05/14/10), http://www.huffingtonpost.com/2010/05/14/baltasar-garzon-spanish-s_n_576 872.html; Scott Horton, "The Poet, the Judge, and the Falangists," http://harpers.org/archive/2010/04/hbc-90006895.

[25]  Kissinger, n. 19 above.

nation struggling to come to terms with a brutal past has a claim as well. The instinct to punish must be related, as in every constitutional democratic political structure, to a system of checks and balances that includes other elements critical to the survival and expansion of democracy.

12. These factors and others[26] not discussed here no doubt have left their imprint in the international law formation process, resulting in the current state of affairs that we will examine in the following pages.

## II. The Reality of Universal Jurisdiction in International Law

13. Reasonable as the idea of universal jurisdiction sounds, persuasive as its logic appears, one must not forget the teaching that "The life of the law has not been logic: it has been experience".[27] The experience and reality of international relations are such that universal jurisdiction over crimes other than piracy has not been established as a matter of international law.

14. An examination of the status of universal jurisdiction in international law is hampered by a lack of clear statement in the relevant primary official materials and a lack of dispassionate and rigorous analyses of them. Over-exaggerated statements expressing support for universal jurisdiction are often found in the writings of various writers. Closer examination, however, may

---

26　See generally Luc Reydams, "The Rise and Fall of Universal Jurisdiction, " Leuven Centre for Global Governance Studies, Working Paper No. 37 ( Leuven Working Paper), http://ghum. kuleuven. be/ggs/publications/working_ papers/new _ series/wp31-40/wp37. pdf, January 2010; papers by George Fletcher, Louise Arbour, Antonio Cassese and Georges Abi-Saab, in *Journal International Criminal Justice* 1 ( 2003), 580-602.

27　O. W. Holmes, The Common Law ( 1886), 1.

lead to differing conclusions. [28] Despite various difficulties, such an examination will be attempted in the following pages under the framework of Article 38 of the ICJ Statute, primarily under paragraph 1 ( a) and 1 ( b), in terms of treaty practice and customary international law. Since there is no dispute about the lawfulness of universal jurisdiction over piracy under international law, I will not deal with piracy in this article.

## Ⅱ. A.  Treaty Practice

15. There are numerous treaties dealing with jurisdiction over crimes of universal concern, presenting a formidable task to any conscientious scholars. Literature also abounds regarding how these treaties should be classified and evaluated. [29] The task is made more difficulty by the controversy surrounding what constitutes universal jurisdiction, properly so called. I will first recap the current discussion of the treaty practice with some commentary of my own and then attempt to sort through these treaties by giving my typological summary of them.

### Ⅱ. A. i.  The Current Evaluation of Treaty Practice

16. The first and most eligible modern crime for pure universal jurisdiction is probably genocide. I believe I need not spill any more ink to prove the

---

28   See generally Luc Reydams, Leuven Working Paper, n. 26 above; id. , Universal Jurisdiction: International and Municipal Legal Perspectives ( 2003); William Schabas, Foreword, ibid.; Zdzislaw Galicki, ILC Special Rapporteur, Fourth report on the obligation to extradite or prosecute ( aut dedere aut judicare), A/CN. 4/648 ( May 31, 2011), http://daccess-dds-ny. un. org/doc/UNDOC /GEN/N11/358/ 84/PDF/N1135884. pdf. For an optimistic assessment of the status of universal jurisdiction in international law, see V. D. Degan and Vesna Baric Punda, Universal Jurisdiction: An Option or a Legal Obligation for States, *International Law Review of Wuhan University* 13 ( 2010): 66-92.

29   See ILC Special Rapporteur, ibid.; Reydams, ibid.

universal concern character of the crime of genocide. Yet, universal jurisdiction over this crime was expressly debated and rejected twice: first when the UNGA drafted and adopted Resolution 96 ( I ) of 1946 and again when it drafted and adopted the Convention for the Prevention and Punishment of the Crime of Genocide ( "Genocide Convention") of 1948. [30] The resultant Article Ⅵ of the Convention relies on the traditional territorial jurisdiction and on a yet to be established international court.

17. Those who claim to have found the existence of universal jurisdiction usually seize upon, as their evidence, the various "extradite or prosecute" provisions in a large number of treaties and assert that these embody the existence of universal jurisdiction. This claim is not supported by a close examination of the treaty practice: although the universal concern character of the crimes dealt with may have motivated the conclusion of these treaties ( a point few would disagree with), the exercise of jurisdiction may be justified on other grounds. "Extradite or prosecute" is a means of exercising jurisdiction; it is not jurisdiction itself. [31] The ways and means of exercising jurisdiction should not be conflated with jurisdiction itself. The "extradite or prosecute" obligation may apply jurisdiction that has been justified on any basis, whether territoriality, nationality, national vital interests or even universal concern. Thus the adoption of this means of exercise of jurisdiction does not necessarily lead to the finding of a particular kind or basis of jurisdiction itself, but of all

---

[30]　See William Schabas, *Genocide in International Law: The Crime of Crimes*, 2nd ed. ( 2009), pp. 49–116, 411–416.

[31]　For another formulation of this difference see AU-EU Expert Report, n. 5 above, para. 11.

the possible kinds utilized.

18. The pivotal point is to identify which kind of jurisdiction that the means ("extradite or prosecute") is utilized to implement. Such an effort reveals no treaty expressly using the "extradite or prosecute" to implement pure universal jurisdiction, and thus no *express* treaty practice support for the idea of pure universal jurisdiction. Having chided the majority for not addressing the issue of jurisdiction and upon an examination of several important treaties, Judges Higgins, Kooijmans and Buergenthal concluded in their Joint Separate Opinion in *Arrest Warrant*[32]:

> 41. The parties to these treaties agreed both to grounds of jurisdiction and as to the obligation to take the measures necessary to establish such jurisdiction. The specified grounds relied on links of nationality of the offender, or the ship or aircraft concerned, or of the victim. See, for example, Article 4 (1), Hague Convention; Article 3 (1), Tokyo Convention; Article 5, Hostages Convention; Article 5, Torture Convention. These may properly be described as treaty-based broad extraterritorial jurisdiction. But in addition to these were the parallel provisions whereby a State party in whose jurisdiction the alleged perpetrator of such offences is found shall prosecute him or extradite him. By the loose use of language the latter has come to be referred to as "universal jurisdiction", though this is really an obligatory territorial jurisdiction over persons, albeit in relation to acts committed elsewhere.

19. Whether the situation where a suspect's presence alone in the

---

[32] Joint Separate Opinion, n. 17 above, 74-75, para. 41.

prosecuting State that refuses to extradite him or her, whose disputed acts had no link to that State, justifies the exercise of jurisdiction is merely what was described by Judge Higgins, et al. , or in fact universal jurisdiction or a conditional form of universal jurisdiction appears to be unsettled. This "mere presence" subsequent to the alleged crime situation is apparently what was contemplated in the provisions on the repression of "grave breaches" of the Geneva Conventions of 1949 [Articles 49 ( I ) ] [33]; 50 ( II ); 129 ( III ); 146 ( IV ); 85 [ AP ( I ) ]. The ICRC in various statements apparently considered this regime to be one of universal jurisdiction. [34] The ICRC Study on the status

---

[33]　That article states in relevant part: "The High Contracting Parties undertake to enact any legislation necessary to provide effective penal sanctions for persons committing, or ordering to be committed, any of the grave breaches of the present Convention defined in the following Article. Each High Contracting Party shall be under the obligation to search for persons alleged to have committed, or to have ordered to be committed, such grave breaches, and shall bring such persons, regardless of their nationality, before its own courts. It may also, if it prefers, and in accordance with the provisions of its own legislation, hand such persons over for trial to another High Contracting Party concerned, provided such High Contracting Party has made out a *prima facie* case. "

The term "search for" can be properly interpreted as "search for persons said to be present on its territory". See Jean S. Pictet's commentary, Convention ( I ) for the Amelioration of the Condition of the Wounded and Sick in Armed Forces in the Field, Geneva, August 12, 1949 ( 1952), 365 – 366 ( http: // www. icrc. org/ihl. nsf/COM/365-570060? OpenDocument).

[34]　Statement by the ICRC representative in the 6th Committee, A/C. 6/65/SR. 12 ( October 15, 2010), 6, para. 42; ICRC Official Statement, 27 – 08 – 2003, on the "First Meeting of Experts of States Parties to the Biological and Toxin Weapons Convention, Geneva, 18 – 29 August 2003 ", http: // www. icrc. org/web/eng/ siteeng0. nsf/htmlall/5qkdpf ( " It should be recalled that States are already required to exercise universal jurisdiction in respect of ' grave breaches' ( of) the 1949 Geneva Conventions and their Additional Protocol I of 1977, which refer to acts committed in situations of armed conflict against protected persons such as wilful killing, torture or inhuman treatment including biological experiments, and making the civilian population or individual civilians the object of attack. Use of biological weapons amounting to such ' grave breaches' would thus require the assertion of universal jurisdiction. " ).

of the customary international humanitarian law also seems to believe so. [35] Expressed in another context[36] or in other ways, [37] some governments also seem to treat this situation as "universal jurisdiction".

20. This view apparently also receives the endorsement of the IDI. During the debate on the universal jurisdiction project, the IDI Rapporteur put emphasis on the lack of a link between the crime and the prosecuting State as the criterion for finding universal jurisdiction. [38] Such "mere presence" was apparently not considered to furnish such a link. The final text of the 2005 IDI resolution in paragraph 2 states:

> Universal jurisdiction is primarily based on customary international law. It can also be established under a multilateral treaty in the relations between the contracting parties, in particular by virtue of clauses which provide that a State party in the territory of which an alleged offender is found shall either extradite or try that person. [39]

The second sentence mentioned above was adopted despite the objections of some members including Higgins and Abi-Saab. [40]

---

[35] See Jean-Marie Henckaerts & Louise Doswald-Beck ( eds. ), *Customary International Humanitarian Law* ( *"ICRC Study"*) 1, Rule 157 and the associated support in vol. 2.

[36] See views of governments as characterized in E/CN. 4/1983/63, paras. 22 & 23, on the proposed Convention against Torture.

[37] See generally the views of the UK government, as quoted in Ian Brownlie, Principles of Public International Law, 7th ed. ( 2008 ), 305-306.

[38] IDI Annuaire, n. 4 above, 257; 261 ( Rapporteur).

[39] IDI Resolution, n. 3 above.

[40] IDI, 71 ( Ⅱ ) Annuaire, n. 4 above, 209-210 ( Abi-Saab); 257 ( Higgins).

21. Furthermore, some treaties require that the alleged crimes have significant links to *some* parties to a particular treaty such as territoriality or nationality; these links to the regime as a whole definitely disqualify the "mere presence" situation as an exercise of truly universal jurisdiction. This would be "universal concern plus treaty, presence and intra-regime territoriality or nationality jurisdiction" as highlighted above. Such a situation is a quintessential intra-regime cooperative affair, in the sense that at least one party to the regime can legitimately exercise jurisdiction based on a traditional criterion, and the prosecuting State party is simply performing the function of that other party in its stead, for whatever reason ( such as its inability or unwillingness to do so). The regime in essence allows the parties to share their traditional jurisdictional powers, or permits one party to exercise the jurisdictional authority of another party. The Geneva Conventions use broadly worded language ("regardless of their nationality") to describe the "extradite or prosecute" obligation, but the application of those Conventions may— though this is not clear—require that the alleged crime was committed on the territory of one of the parties to the Conventions, thus requiring a first level connection ( such as nationality, territoriality, victim nationality, or vital interests) with at least one party to the applicable Convention. In any event, subsequently treaties such as the Convention against Torture and Other Cruel, Inhuman or Degrading Treatment or Punishment of 1984 make it clearer that the "mere presence" of a suspect in the territory of one of the parties is of a secondary nature; the crime or the suspect must have a first level link such as territoriality or nationality with one of the parties to the

Convention for the suspect to be subject to some kind of process. This is at least one plausible reading of article 5 of the Convention against Torture. That article reads:

Article 5

1. Each State Party shall take such measures as may be necessary to establish its jurisdiction over the offences referred to in article 4 in the following cases:

(a) When the offences are committed in any territory under its jurisdiction or on board a ship or aircraft registered in that State;

(b) When the alleged offender is a national of that State;

(c) When the victim is a national of that State if that State considers it appropriate.

2. Each State Party shall likewise take such measures as may be necessary to establish its jurisdiction over such offences in cases where the alleged offender is present in any territory under its jurisdiction and it does not extradite him pursuant to article 8 to any of the States mentioned in paragraph 1 of this article.

3. This Convention does not exclude any criminal jurisdiction exercised in accordance with internal law.

Paragraph 1 of this article provides for the obligation to establish jurisdiction based on territoriality, nationality or victim nationality. Paragraph 2 provides for the obligation to prosecute if the suspect is not extradited to "any of the States mentioned in paragraph 1 of this article". One reading of this provision would be that for paragraph 2 to apply, paragraph 1 must have been potentially applicable but the requested State is not willing to extradite the suspect; that is to say, the suspect or the suspected crime must have first level links to a State party ("any State mentioned in paragraph 1", which deals with States parties only)—territoriality, nationality or victim nationality—to establish that potential applicability. So read, article 5 (2) does not deal with matters outside the province of the regime.

22. A further and clearer illustration of this regime is the Rome Statute of the International Criminal Court, which in article 12 provides for the ICC— which can be considered a cooperative of the States Parties—to take jurisdiction based on a territoriality link between the crime and a State party or a nationality link between the suspect and a State party.

23. One may argue that there can be an alternative and broader reading of article 49 of Geneva Convention ( I ) and the corresponding articles in the other Geneva Conventions as well as article 5 (2) of the Convention against Torture. This alternative reading would not require first level links between the suspect or the suspected crime and a State party for the "extradite or prosecute" obligation to be triggered. Indeed, article 49 of Geneva Convention ( I ) is so broadly written that it may be susceptible of the alternative reading. Further, one can imagine a reading of article 5 (2) of the Convention against Torture this way: that paragraph 2 is triggered whenever a suspect is not extradited to any State party, irrespective of the reasons for that. Under this reading, whether or not paragraph 1 is potentially applicable is immaterial, although if it is not applicable, it will be because the suspect is a

national of a third State accused of a crime occurring on the territory of a third State against a national of a third State and is not extradited to any State party. However, this reading would seem to render part of the language of article 5 ( 2 ) redundant or unnaturally formulated. If such an alternative reading is accepted, this situation would be the "universal concern plus treaty and presence jurisdiction" as highlighted above.

24. Other examples of this situation include article 4 ( 2 ) of the 1970 Hague Convention for the Suppression of Unlawful Seizure of Aircraft[41] and

---

41    See Joint Separate Opinion, *ICJ Reports 2002*, 73, para. 35;  President Guillaume, Separate Opinion, in his separate opinion, ibid. , 38, para. 7. There President Guillaume emphasized the obligation to establish jurisdiction so that "the obligation to prosecute was no longer conditional on the existence of jurisdiction on, but rather jurisdiction itself had to be established in order to make prosecution possible", and he seemed to call this "compulsory, albeit subsidiary, universal jurisdiction". He took as the forerunner Article 4 ( 2 ) of the Hague Convention for the Suppression of Unlawful Seizure of Aircraft of 1970. One may agree with this emphasis if the obligation to establish jurisdiction cannot be considered a logical extension of, or as included in, the term "extradite or prosecute". To prosecute implies the existence of the wherewithal to do so, i. e. , the establishment of jurisdiction. In any event, a general promise to take effective measures to repress crimes would have included such an obligation. This is the understanding of the broadly worded Article 49, especially paragraph 1, of the Geneva Convention ( I ) of 1949 and the corresponding articles in the other Geneva Conventions. Furthermore, Article 4 ( 2 ) of the Hague Convention for the Suppression of Unlawful Seizure of Aircraft of 1970 expressly requires the presence of the suspect on the territory of the Contracting State, while Article 49 of the Geneva Convention has been construed as requiring the same. That is to say, potentially the 1970 Hague Convention may not be the first on the requirement to establish jurisdiction.

article V of the Apartheid Convention. [42] Both can be read as authorizing the exercise of jurisdiction over a suspect, a national of a third State, who is present in the prosecuting State party to the applicable convention for crimes that have occurred in a third State. We cannot be certain that this reading is correct, there does not appear to be any record of these provisions being applied this way either administrative or judicially.

25. However, even this "universal concern plus treaty and presence jurisdiction" is not true or pure universal jurisdiction, as a treaty permission or obligation to exercise jurisdiction and the presence of the suspect are required. Only when a treaty claims to give the parties thereto jurisdiction over crimes and suspects having no link with any of the parties to the treaty, one would see pure universal jurisdiction. For example, if the 1970 Hague Convention would authorize jurisdiction over a national of a third party to the Convention who is not yet present in the prosecuting State party to the Convention for crimes occurring in a third State, that would present a "pure

---

[42]  Apartheid Convention, art. V, which states: "Persons charged with the acts enumerated in article II of the present Convention may be tried by a competent tribunal of any State Party to the Convention which may acquire jurisdiction over the person of the accused or by an international penal tribunal having jurisdiction with respect to those States Parties which shall have accepted its jurisdiction. " "Acquire jurisdiction over the person of the accused" is not clear, but in my view apparently means his or her presence. This Convention is quite special both in terms of the circumstances of adoption and the political climate prevailing then. See comment by John Dugard, http: //untreaty. un. org/cod/avl/pdf/ha/cspca/ cspca_e. pdf, 2 ("The Apartheid Convention allows State parties to prosecute non-nationals for a crime committed in the territory of a non-State party where the accused is physically within the jurisdiction of a State party (arts. 4 and 5). (...) No one was prosecuted for the crime of apartheid while apartheid lasted in South Africa. And no one has since been prosecuted for the crime. "). But cf. Reydams, Leuven Working Paper, n. 26 above, 18, who seemed to characterize the Apartheid Convention, art. V, as granting universal jurisdiction.

universal concern jurisdiction" scenario. However, no such a treaty is readily found, although I have not done exhaustive research on this. The Judges in the *Arrest Warrant* case (especially those who issued opinions on the issue of universal jurisdiction) and the various scholars who have done thorough research on universal jurisdiction have not reported one either.

26. The phrasing of some treaty provisions may give rise to the impression or the argument that the treaty somehow impliedly recognizes universal jurisdiction. For example, the Second Protocol to the Hague Convention for the Protection of Cultural Property in the Event of Armed Conflict (1999), [43] in article 16 (2) (a), states that the Protocol "does not preclude [ …] the exercise of jurisdiction under national and international law that may be applicable, or affect the exercise of jurisdiction under customary international law". The ICRC experts on customary international humanitarian law were of the view that

The Second Protocol to the Hague Convention for the Protection of Cultural Property states that it does not affect "the exercise of jurisdiction under customary international law", which was intended by delegates at the negotiation of the Protocol to refer to the right of States to vest universal jurisdiction in their national courts for war crimes. [44]

The experts did not present evidence from drafting history.

_____

43   http://portal. unesco. org/en/ev. php-URL_ID = 15207&URL_ DO = DO_ TO PIC&URL_ SECTION = 201. html.

44   *ICRC Study*, n. 35 above, vol. 1, 605, & n. 198.

27. It is better not to read this provision this way; it is better to read it as a provision preventing an *a contrario* interpretation of article 16 that it prohibits other forms of exercises of jurisdiction not spelled out in the article. It would be a jump to read it as supporting a particular form of exercise such as universal jurisdiction. Such a meaning would have required affirmative support in the text of the treaty itself. This better interpretation is supported by the similar interpretation generally given to article 5 (3) of the Convention against Torture. [45]

## II. A. ii. Summary of Treaty Practice

28. The messy treaty practice and scholarly treatment do not afford much confidence in us when we attempt to distill any rules of customary international law from it. The universal concern character of the crimes under consideration may have motivated the conclusion of a substantial number of treaties, but whatever we would like to say about these treaties, it will be advisable for us to remember that a treaty right or obligation is only applicable to the parties thereto and is subject to a variety of conditions specific to that treaty. [46] Nevertheless, data do show that there is no instance of "pure universal concern jurisdiction" being authorized in any treaty. Some treaties authorize or can be interpreted as authorizing "universal concern plus treaty and presence jurisdiction". Even more treaties authorize "universal concern plus treaty, presence and intra-regime territoriality or nationality jurisdiction".

---

[45]　See Joint Separate Opinion, Arrest Warrant, above n. 17, paras. 34, 38.

[46]　See Statement of China ( Chinese original at: http://www. un. org/en/ga/sixth/65/ScopeApp UniJuri_ StatesComments/China. pdf; English translation by the UN at: http://www. un. org/en/ga/sixth/ 65/ScopeApp UniJuri_ StatesComments/China_ E. pdf) , Observations, para. 6.

But neither of the latter two types can be properly called "universal jurisdiction".

## II. B. Customary International Law

29. Turning to the customary international law status of universal jurisdiction, one is of course reminded of the requirements as stated in article 38 ( 1 ) ( b ) of the ICJ Statute for the finding of such a rule: customary international law is evidenced by a general State practice accepted as law ( i. e. , *opinio juris*) .

30. In this regard, one is struck by the lack of evidence of clear exercise of "pure universal concern" jurisdiction and the seemingly broad support for "universal jurisdiction", loosely described, as evidenced in the various declarations and statements. If the latter were to be taken at face value, there appears to be *opinio juris* for the concept of "universal jurisdiction", loosely used, over genocide, crimes against humanity and serious war crimes. For example, as early as in 1971, a General Assembly resolution was broadly worded so as to be consistent with the idea of universal jurisdiction. There, the GA "*affirms* that refusal by States to cooperation in the arrest, extradition, trial and punishment of persons guilty of war crimes and crimes against humanity is contrary to the purposes and principles of the Charter of the United Nations and to generally recognized norms of international law".[47] Many Western States have made statements supporting the concept of universal jurisdiction. [48] The African Union stated, in a memorandum annexed

---

[47] UNGA Res 2840 ( 1971) .

[48] For further info, see AU-EU Expert Report, n. 5 above; *ICRC Study*, n. 35 above.

to the request for the inclusion of universal jurisdiction in the agenda of the 63$^{rd}$ session of the UNGA, that "The principle of universal jurisdiction is well established in international law" and that "The African Union respects this principle, which is enshrined in article 4 ( h) of the Constitutive Act" but that it was concerned about the uncertain scope and application of the principle and the abuse of it. [49] The American Law Institute, a national institute of legal experts, found that universal jurisdiction existed under customary international law over several crimes as early as 1986. [50] The IDI, a world academy of international law experts, also gave its support to the concept or principle of universal jurisdiction in 2005. [51]

31. In any event, data on State conduct asserting universal jurisdiction do not reveal sufficient evidence establishing true universal jurisdiction, other than in cases of piracy. This is more or less the conclusion of the Western judges including Judges Higgins, Kooijmans, Buergenthal, and President Guillaume in *Arrest Warrant* ( 2002). The Joint Separate Opinion by Higgins, Kooijmans and Buergenthal in *Arrest Warrant* endorsed[52] the opinion of the authors of *Oppenheim's International Law* ( 9th ed. , 1996, 998), that:

While no general rule of positive international law can as yet be asserted

---

49　A/63/237, annex ( Explanatory memorandum), para. 1. The States of the Non-aligned Movement seemed to hold a more ambiguous attitude. See A/C. 6/64/SR. 12 ( November 25, 2009), paras. 20-21; A/C. 6/65/SR. 10 ( October 13, 2010), paras. 55-56.

50　ALI, Restatement of the Law, Third, the Foreign Relations of the United States, § 404 and the comments and notes thereto. The text is reproduced in n. 7 above.

51　IDI Resolution, n. 3 above.

52　Joint Separate Opinion, n. 17 above, para. 52.

which gives rise to states the right to punish foreign nationals for crimes against humanity in the same way as they are, for instance, entitled to punish acts of piracy, there are clear indications pointing to the gradual evolution of a significant principle of international law to that effect.

Subsequent development has not strengthened the status of universal jurisdiction; rather, it has weakened it, as discussed below, especially in paragraph 34. In a sense, the fortune of universal jurisdiction peaked in 2002 when *Arrest Warrant* was decided.

32. Although some States such as the United Kingdom[53] have asserted universal jurisdiction over war crimes in their military law or regulations in the form of manuals, this assertion does not appear to have attracted general following among States, or have extended to other crimes or to other prosecuting contexts. Indeed, the United Kingdom's military manual even has difficulty persuading its own legislature to implement that idea by statute, [54] and a "clever" solution was found to implement the Rome Statute. The ICRC Study seems to have a broader view of the exercise of "universal jurisdiction" over war crimes. [55] A critical analysis of the data presented may not bear out its assessment.

---

[53] British Manual of Military Law, III (1956), para. 637, as quoted in Rosalyn Higgins, Problems and Process (1994), 59–60; see discussion of id., 56–61; Ian Brownlie, Principles of Public International Law (7th ed., 2008), 305–306; UK Ministry of Defence, The Manual of the Law of Armed Conflict (2004), para. 16. 30.

[54] See Ian Brownlie, Principles of Public International Law, 7th ed. (2008), 305 – 306; Rosalyn Higgins, *Problems and Process* (1994), 59–61.

[55] See *ICRC Study*, n. 35 above, Rule 157 and the associated materials.

33. The German legislations including the Code of Crimes against Humanity Law in a complicated way have been considered by one commentator to allow for the possibility of pure universal jurisdiction, [56] with various conditions. This possibility remains a possibility even now, as no such prosecution has been made.

34. The limited support from national legislation for true universal jurisdiction has recently been further diminished. In 2003 and 2009 respectively, Belgium[57] and Spain, [58] the only two States, as commonly believed, that once had clear statutes asserting pure universal jurisdiction and have in fact attempted to exercise that jurisdiction ( Germany is not because of the ambiguities in its legislations and its record of non-exercise), have now modified their statutes to condition the exercise of jurisdiction on various links with the forum State.

35. The limited cases from the Western States regarding the attempt to exercise or actual exercise of universal jurisdiction have been described as showing the courts had "largely been cautious so far as reliance on universal

---

56　See the description and analysis of this law in Luc Reydams, *Universal Jurisdiction* ( 2003) , 141-147.

57　5 August, 2003 Act on Grave Breaches of International Humanitarian Law ( Belgium) . See Luc Reydams, Belgium Reneges on Universality: 5 August, 2003 Act on Grave Breaches of International Humanitarian Law, *Journal International Criminal Justice* 1 ( 2003) : 679-689.

58　Ley Orgánica 1/2009, de 3 de noviembre complementaria de la Ley de reforma de la legislación procesal para la implantación de la nueva Oficina judicial, por la que se modifica la Ley Orgánica 6/1985, de 1 de julio, del Poder Judicial ( http://noticias. juridicas. com/base_ datos/Admin/lol-2009. html) ( Spain). The essence of this new law, as stated by representative of Spain in the UNGA, A/C. 6/65/ SR. 11, October 13, 2010, 4, para. 21, is: " judges could only prosecute perpetrators of serious crimes committed anywhere in the world when no other international or third-country court had initiated proceedings against them and when they were present in Spanish territory or when the victim was a Spanish national."

jurisdiction is concerned". [59] Alternatively, this situation has been described in 2010 by Reydams [60] as follows:

All in all some two dozen individuals have been tried by courts in Austria, Canada, Germany, Denmark, Belgium, the United Kingdom, the Netherlands, Finland, France, Spain, and Switzerland for "war crimes" committed abroad. Without exception the defendants had taken up permanent residence in the forum state—as refugee, exile, fugitive, or immigrant—and resisted being "sent back to the countries in which their abominable deeds were done". In most cases the other states concerned acquiesced in or even supported prosecution. Not to overlook also is the fact that the majority of these cases concerned atrocities committed in the former Yugoslavia and in Rwanda; the prosecutor of the ad hoc international criminal tribunals for these countries and the UN Security Council had encouraged all states to search for and try suspects on their territory (cf. the obligations under the Geneva Conventions). Finally, extradition often was impossible, if not legally then practically.

In addition, the rare examples of express assertion of universal jurisdiction

---

59 See the analysis in the Joint Separate Opinion, n. 17 above, para. 21.

60 Luc Reydams, Leuven Working Paper, n. 26 above, 22 (internal footnotes omitted). See also the description of State judicial practice in: The Scope and application of the principle of universal jurisdiction: Report of the Secretary-General prepared on the basis comments and observations of Governments, A/65/181, July 29, 2010, http://daccess-dds-ny. un. org/doc/UNDOC/GE N/N10/467/52/PDF/N1046752. pdf?OpenElement), paras. 55-65; 94-107.

from Israel (*Eichmann*[61]) and United States (*Demjanjuk,* [62] recognizing Israel's universal jurisdiction as a basis for extradition) have their value reduced by the special circumstances surrounding these prosecutions of perpetrators from the Nazi era and further by Israel's threats against the use of universal jurisdiction against its own officials and the claim of the United States that other States *"should not even think about"*[63] prosecuting its nationals.

36. Finally, it should be noted that no African State has ever exercised universal jurisdiction. [64]

37. But the IDI seems to believe that universal jurisdiction exists under customary international law but it finds it to be conditional on the "presence" of the suspect, as described below. [65] One may find the IDI Resolution extraordinary, as it was passed in 2005 against the background of the *Arrest*

---

61    *AG of Israel v Eichmann*, 36 ILR 5 ( District Court of Jerusalem, 1961) and 277 ( Supreme Court of Israel, 1962) .

62    In re Demjanjuk, 603 F. Supp. 1468 ( ND Ohio) , affirmed, 776 F. 2d 571 ( 6th Cir. 1985) , cert. denied, 457 US 1016 ( 1986) .

63    Reydams, Leuven Working Paper, n. 26 above, 22.

64    AU-EU Expert Report, n. 5 above, paras. 19, 26, 40.

65    IDI Resolution, n. 3 above.

*Warrant* Judgment arresting the over-enthusiasm for universal jurisdiction[66] and Belgium, the captain of universal jurisdiction, abandoning ship by modifying pure universal jurisdiction out of its statute in 2003. [67] That is to say, the trend in favor of pure universal jurisdiction, if at all, was reversing. In any event, the IDI Resolution did not arrest the reversing trend so far, and in 2009 Spain did what Belgium did in 2003. [68]

38. It will be better for us to analyze these cases one by one, but the conscientious judges and scholars have done so and given conflicting assessments of the record. This alone reflects the uncertain state of universal jurisdiction in international law.

39. This state of affairs appears to be susceptible of several interpretations. First of all, the lack of actual exercise of pure universal jurisdiction may be considered to be evidence showing that the nice-sounding support for the concept is really political, rather than evidencing *opinio juris*.

---

66    After the Congo reformulated its claims, the ICJ did not rule in *Arrest Warrant* on the lawfulness of universal jurisdiction; rather, it held that it was unable to find any customary international law exception to the immunity from foreign national jurisdiction and the inviolability that an incumbent foreign minister enjoys, even where that foreign minister is accused of having committed war crimes or crimes against humanity. On the effect of Arrest Warrant, see Alain Pellet, Shaping the Future of International Law: The Role of the World Court in Law-making, in: Mahnoush H. Arsanjani, et al. ( eds. ), Looking to the Future: Essays on International Law in Honor of W. Michael Reisman ( 2011), 1065, 1080 ( "the ICJ's Judgment in *Arrest Warrant Case* shows that the Court can also slow down and maybe go as far as durably jeopardizing highly desirable evolutions in the law in force"); Antonio Cassese, n. 26 above, 1 J Int'l Criminal Justice, 589-595. On immunities ( not discussed in this paper), see, e. g. , the reports of the ILC Special Rapporteur Roman Anatolevich Kolodkin and other materials, available at: http://untreaty. un. org/ilc/guide/4 _ 2. htm.

67    See n. 57 above.

68    See n. 58 above.

40. The support of the African Union as stated in its 2009 memorandum for this concept is further weakened by its expressed reliance on article 4 ( h ) of its Constitutive Act, [69] which, the African Union statement claims, "enshrine [ s ]"[70] the principle of universal jurisdiction. That article recognizes "the right of the Union to intervene in a Member State pursuant to a decision of the Assembly in respect of grave circumstances, namely: war crimes, genocide and crimes against humanity". This article in fact enshrines an intra-regime collective political action mechanism: it grants the right to the Union to take action in relevant situations, not to any individual State to take action; the action authorized is political collective enforcement action, not judicial enforcement action. It does not say anything about the Union's right to exercise universal jurisdiction, much less that of an individual State to exercise universal jurisdiction. These factors may not have received attention when the statement of the African Union States was formulated.

41. The exchange of views by States so far after the inclusion of universal jurisdiction on the agenda of the UNGA does not strengthen the status of universal jurisdiction. The number of States that have submitted statements to the UNGA is not substantial, only 44 in total, about 25% of the membership of

---

69　Text accompany n. 49 above.

70　African Union memo, n. 1 above, para. 1.

the UN. [71] Nor has this exchange clarified much, as broad and loose language seems to continue to prevail. If anything, this exercise seems to lessen the meager support for the concept. Several States have noted that "the scope and application of universal jurisdiction remained very much a matter of political and legal debate".[72] Some States such as Thailand[73] have made clear statements arguing against universal jurisdiction over crimes other than piracy and/or slavery. Even the African Union which clearly expressed support for the "principle" of universal jurisdiction in 2009 seemed to have retreated in 2010 from its earlier position. The statement made on behalf the African Group of States before the 6th Committee in October 2010 said:

There was as yet no generally accepted definition of universal jurisdiction and no agreement on which crimes, other than piracy and slavery, it should cover or on the conditions under which it would apply. If few States had responded with information about their practice on universal

---

[71] The statements are available on line here: http://www. un. org/en/ga /sixth/65/ScopeApp UniJuri. shtml. For a summary by these statements, see The Scope and application of the principle of universal jurisdiction: Report of the Secretary-General prepared on the basis comments and observations of Governments, A/65/181 ( July 29, 2010), http://daccess-dds-ny. un. org/doc/ UNDOC/GEN/N10/467/ 52/PDF/N1046752. pdf?OpenElement. In 2010 China submitted a statement ( Statement of China, n. 46 above). See also ZHU Lijiang, Chinese Practice in Public International Law: 2009, *Chinese Journal of International Law* 9 ( 2010):607, 647, para. 75.

[72] See, e. g. , statement of Malaysia, A/C. 6/65/SR. 12 ( October 15, 2010), 5, para. 26.

[73] See, e. g. , statement of Thailand, A/C. 6/65/SR. 11 ( October 13, 2010), 3, para. 12 ( "With the exception of piracy, there was no general consensus among States as to which crimes were subject to universal jurisdiction under customary international law. "); Sudan, A/C. 6/65/SR. 12 ( October 15, 2010), 4, para. 20; statement of China, n. 46 above.

jurisdiction, it was because the principle hardly existed in most domestic jurisdictions. [74]

Furthermore, rather than reiterating that the Constitutive Act of the African Union " enshrined " the principle of universal jurisdiction, the statement now said that "the Constitutive Act of the African Union accorded the Union the power to intervene in the affairs of its member States in situations of genocide, war crimes and crimes against humanity". [75]

42. Secondly, the thin record of actual exercise is evidence that there is no positive rule of customary international law yet in favor of pure universal jurisdiction other than that over piracy. [76] Indeed, there is not even sufficient evidence to prove a customary international law rule permitting the exercise of "universal concern plus presence" jurisdiction.

43. Finally, another interpretation, as put forward in the Joint Separate Opinion of Judge Higgins, et al. in *Arrest Warrant*, is that this only shows that States have not "( legislated) to the full scope of the jurisdiction allowed by international law" and that:

> While none of the national case law to which [ the Judges] have referred happens to be based on the exercise of a universal jurisdiction properly so called, there is equally nothing in this case law which evidences an *opinio*

---

[74] A/C. 6/65/SR. 10 ( October 13, 2010), http://daccess-ods. un. org/access. nsf/Get? Open&DS = A/C. 6/65/SR. 10&Lang = E, para. 60.

[75] Ibid. , para. 61.

[76] See Statement of China, n. 46 above, Observations, paras. 4-5.

*juris* on the illegality of such a jurisdiction. In short, national legislation and case law—that is, State practice—is neutral as to exercise of universal jurisdiction. [77]

## III. Possible application of the *Lotus* dictum

44. Concluding thus, the Joint Separate Opinion by Judge Higgins, et al. in *Arrest Warrant* argued in essence that the matter then turns on not whether the exercise of true or pure universal jurisdiction is supported by positive international law, but whether such an exercise is precluded by any prohibitive rule, in application of the *Lotus* dictum which militates in favor of state freedom. Finding no such prohibitive rule, these Judges concluded that a State may exercise pure universal jurisdiction ( or "universal jurisdiction *in absentia*") . [78]

45. President Guillaume, on the other hand, directly challenged the very dictum itself, at least in its application to the area of criminal jurisdiction. He said in his Separate Opinion in *Arrest Warrant* [79]:

---

77　Joint Separate Opinion, n. 17 above, para. 45. The UK explanation is found in Rosalyn Higgins, *Problems and Process* ( 1994) , 59–61.

78　See Joint Separate Opinion, n. 17 above, paras. 49–54, etc.

79　President Guillaume, Separate Opinion in Arrest Warrant, *ICJ Reports 2002*, 35, 43. For further criticisms of the *Lotus* dictum, see Judge Simma, Declaration, in Accordance with International Law of the Unilateral Declaration of Independence in Respect of Kosovo ( Request for Advisory Opinion) , *ICJ Reports 2010*, http://www. icj-cij. org/docket/files/141/1599 3. pdf; Sienho Yee, Notes on the International Court of Justice ( Part 4) : The Kosovo Advisory Opinion, *Chinese Journal of International Law* 9 ( 2010) : 763, paras. 22–26.

14. This argument is hardly persuasive. Indeed the Permanent Court itself, having laid down the general principle cited by Belgium, then asked itself "whether the foregoing considerations really apply as regards criminal jurisdiction". It held that either this might be the case, or alternatively, that: "the exclusively territorial character of law relating to this domain constitutes a principle which, except as otherwise expressly provided, would, *ipso facto*, prevent States from extending the criminal jurisdiction of their courts beyond their frontiers". In the particular case before it, the Permanent Court took the view that it was unnecessary to decide the point. Given that the case involved the collision of a French vessel with a Turkish vessel, the Court confined itself to noting that the effects of the offence in question had made themselves felt on Turkish territory, and that consequently a criminal prosecution might "be justified from the point of view of this so-called territorial principle".

15. The absence of a decision by the Permanent Court on the point was understandable in 1927, given the sparse treaty law at that time. The situation is different today, it seems to me—totally different. The adoption of the United Nations Charter proclaiming the sovereign equality of States, and the appearance on the international scene of new States, born of decolonization, have strengthened the territorial principle. International criminal law has itself undergone considerable development and constitutes today an impressive legal *corpus*. It recognizes in many situations the possibility, or indeed the obligation, for a State other than that on whose territory the offence was committed to confer jurisdiction on its courts to prosecute the authors of certain crimes where they are present on its territory. International criminal courts have been created. But at no time has it been

envisaged that jurisdiction should be conferred upon the courts of every State in the world to prosecute such crimes, whoever their authors and victims and irrespective of the place where the offender is to be found. To do this would, moreover, risk creating total judicial chaos. It would also be to encourage the arbitrary for the benefit of the powerful, purportedly acting as agent for an ill-defined "international community". Contrary to what is advocated by certain publicists, such a development would represent not an advance in the law but a step backward.

46. There is much force in President Guillaume's view. The *Lotus* dictum was indeed unnecessary in that case and its vitality results from the uncritical recitation to and following of it.

47. To some extent, the debate seems to be about which default rule is the proper one. When the decision was adopted by the Permanent Court of International Justice, States still adhered to the old rule of a right to use of force to settle international disputes. It was probably natural that State freedom was considered paramount and therefore given priority. That apparently was the default rule behind the application of the *Lotus* dictum. In any event, developments since the date of the decision in 1927 militate against following it anymore. Since the first renunciation of the use of force as an instrument of national policy in the Kellogg-Briand Pact of Paris of 1928 and the restatement of this position in Article 2 (4) of the UN Charter, State freedom is now subordinated to the territorial integrity and political independence of States. This is now the grand default rule for the entire international legal system. In the words of President Guillaume, these new

developments have strengthened the territorial principle. The *Lotus* dictum therefore can be considered outdated at least as far as criminal jurisdiction is concerned. This is also the view of some IDI members[80] expressed during its deliberations leading to the adoption of the 2005 Resolution on the topic. Indeed, in some areas States have positively by treaty reversed the holding of the PCIJ in *Lotus* regarding criminal jurisdiction. [81]

48. Rejecting the *Lotus* dictum in this context, China expressly states in its statement submitted to the UNGA in 2010 on universal jurisdiction:

> Jurisdiction is an important element of State sovereignty. Under the principle of sovereign equality of States, the establishment and exercise of [jurisdiction] by one State may not impair the sovereignty of other States. Therefore the establishment of a State's [jurisdiction] should have as a prerequisite the existence of valid and adequate connections between that country and the cases involved, and should be limited to a reasonable scope. [82]

49. One cannot but await further development on this point with great interest. Before the *Lotus* dictum is defeated in this area, conceivably the States may prevent its application by making objections to universal jurisdiction, because the basis for its application, according to the Joint

---

80　See IDI, 71 ( II ) Annuaire, n. 4 above, 245 ( The Rapporteur) ; 258 ( Frowein).

81　E. g. , 1952 Brussels Convention for the Unification of Certain Rules Relating to Penal Jurisdiction in Matters of Collision or other Incidents of Navigation, art. 1; UNCLOS, art. 97.

82　Statement of China, n. 46 above, Observations, para. 1, English translation by the UN. This UN translation mistakenly translates "guanxiaquan" into "sovereignty". "Jurisdiction" is used here instead.

Separate Opinion in *Arrest Warrant*, is the fact that there is nothing that evinces an *opinio juris* on the illegality of universal jurisdiction. A State's silent non-support alone for universal jurisdiction will not necessarily prevent it from being applied to the nationals of that State, as the effect of the application of the *Lotus* dictum is such that it may permit a State's exercise of jurisdiction not authorized, but not prohibited either, by international law. This means that making clear objections has its benefits, while "diplomatic" ambiguity or silence may have its perils as far as the application of the *Lotus* dictum is concerned.

## IV. Possible Limitations on the Exercise of Universal Jurisdiction if Permitted

50. From the above analysis, we can see that universal jurisdiction may be a positive tool in the efforts to vindicate the fundamental values of the international community, to promote and protect human rights and to fight impunity. Its negative side is that the exercise of universal jurisdiction is at least in tension with the principle of sovereignty and sovereign equality and is easily subjected to political abuse including discrimination as manifested in selective prosecution, thus destabilizing international relations. [83] If one were to assume, *arguendo*, that this doctrine or principle could be used for whatever reason and to attempt to reap the benefits of the tool while reducing its side effects, one can imagine that the exercise of universal jurisdiction may be placed under a variety of conditions or whether such conditions should be

---

83  See Henry Kissinger, n. 19 above.

made part of the "definition" of universal jurisdiction, such as ( 1 ) limiting that exercise to the most heinous crimes such as, in addition to piracy, slavery, genocide, crimes against humanity and serious war crimes; ( 2 ) giving priority to the territorial State, ( 3 ) applying the clean-hands doctrine; [84] ( 4 ) requiring a decision of the highest State authority to trigger the exercise; ( 5 ) respecting applicable immunities of officials and States; ( 6 ) possible approval of an international screening mechanism; and ( 7 ) the presence of the suspect. These are not discussed herein, except that I will make some comments on the presence requirement or condition.

51. It seems that there is broad support for the point that there is no customary international law rule allowing the exercise of universal jurisdiction without the presence of the suspect. [85] There is insufficient support for the view that the presence of the suspect would legitimize the exercise of "universal jurisdiction", absent support from a treaty. Furthermore, there is disagreement on the temporal point at which the presence requirement is triggered, if the exercise of universal jurisdiction is permitted for some reason. It seems that for Judge Higgins, et al. in the *Arrest Warrant* case who still would rely on the *Lotus* dictum, this finding about the role of presence in itself does not show that the presence of the suspect is thereby required for the exercise of universal jurisdiction; for a State to exercise universal jurisdiction, there need be only no prohibitive rule against it. The existence of such a

---

[84]　See Sienho Yee, The *Tu Quoque* Argument as a Defence to International Crimes, Prosecution, or Punishment, *Chinese Journal of International Law* 3 ( 2004 ) : 87–133.

[85]　See statement of Israel, A/C. 6/65/SR. 12, October 15, 2010, 3, para. 9 ( "many States agreed that the accused should be present in the territory of the forum State") .

presence requirement in the various treaty provisions on extradite or prosecute—in their view, "*Definitionally, this envisages presence on the territory*"—is no ground for reaching an *a contrario* conclusion so that the presence is required. [86] For these judges, "If it is said that a person must be within the jurisdiction at the time of the trial itself, that may be a prudent guarantee for the right of fair trial but has little to do with bases of jurisdiction recognized under international law". [87] One cannot but note that this view, reducing the presence requirement to the mere procedural requirement of a prudent guarantee for a fair trial is far reaching and extraordinary against the trend in international criminal law shunning trials *in absentia*. Indeed, this trend may evince a certain attitude about or view of the world we live in, rather than a mere quest for a fairer trial. The far reaching effect of the procedural view of the presence requirement will be greater still—perhaps exponentially so—when it is coupled with the application of the *Lotus* dictum, which the Joint Separate Opinion in *Arrest Warrant* argued for, because both are biased in favor of the freedom of the prosecuting State. [88]

52. According to the IDI and others, the trigger point appears earlier. The IDI Resolution, in paragraph 3 ( b ) , states:

Apart from acts of investigation and requests for extradition, the exercise of universal jurisdiction requires the presence of the alleged offender in the

---

86    Joint Separate Opinion, n. 17 above, in particular, para. 57 ( emphasis in the original ) .

87    Joint Separate Opinion, n. 17 above, para. 56.

88    This has the danger of leading to the maximum freedom of the prosecuting State, a sort of "*Lotus-maximum*", see Sienho Yee, n. 79 above, *Chinese Journal of International Law* 9 ( 2010) : 763, para. 26.

territory of the prosecuting State or on board a vessel flying its flag or an aircraft which is registered under its laws, or other lawful forms of control over the alleged offender.

According to the Rapporteur, this paragraph

rejected the theory of absolute universal jurisdiction, insisting on the presence of the alleged perpetrator on the territory of the prosecuting State. However, it did allow any State to undertake acts of investigation which per se did not harm the individual, unlike the issue of an arrest warrant. Likewise, States should be free to request extradition, although there was no obligation for the requested State to comply with such request. [89]

While this approach is reasonable to some extent, there are still three major problems. The first is this: if the requested State is where the suspect holds an official position, it will probably not comply with an extradition request without a tough decision; if this requested State is one different from the suspect's home State ( when the suspect/official travels outside), different considerations may be entertained and the request for extradition may well be complied with.

53. The second is that existing judicial assistance or extradition treaties may indeed mandate extradition because under at least some of these treaties the requested State may be required to surrender a suspect if the requesting

---

[89]　IDI Annuaire, n. 4 above, 208 ( the Rapporteur introducing the draft resolution) .

State has made out a prima facie case in terms of jurisdiction and evidence and pure universal jurisdiction may be considered sufficient to satisfy that jurisdictional requirement. How to reconcile the IDI Rapporteur's view that the requested State is under no obligation ( resulting from the universal jurisdiction law itself) to comply with such a request and the requested State's obligation to comply under other species of law becomes a most important question. In other words, should there be, in the context of universal jurisdiction, an exception from the general obligation arising from other species of law to comply with requests?

54. Thirdly, in some countries the initiation of an investigation may result in compulsory judicial processes other than arrest and extradition. This lesser form of compulsory judicial processes can still present serious problems. However, arguing for conditioning the starting of an investigation on the presence of the suspect may be too much and will likely be rejected by many States. Perhaps a compromise position can be to condition the issuance of any compulsory judicial process on the presence of the suspect on the territory of the prosecuting State.

55. This discussion should raise a red flag to any cautious government that the relationship between the possible exercise of universal jurisdiction and all the judicial and police assistance treaties and the implications of the presence requirement on this relationship are a subject calling out for urgent examination. It may wish to attempt to modify these treaties to ensure a relaxed presence requirement will not present a problem for its conduct of international relations.

## V. Concluding Remarks

56.True or pure universal jurisdiction is jurisdiction solely based on the universal concern character of the crime in issue. The concept and logic of universal jurisdiction is understandable, as each State has an interest in matters of universal concern. Universal jurisdiction can be a powerful instrument for the international system to protect its interests and to protect human rights and fight against impunity. However, the exercise of universal jurisdiction by one State may infringe the sovereignty and sovereign equality of another State and can be abused, thus destabilizing international relations.

57. These pros and cons and others not discussed here have influenced the international law formation process in such a way that so far only universal jurisdiction over piracy has been accepted in international law. There is insufficient support to show that "pure universal concern jurisdiction" exists in international law over other crimes yet. The evidence of State practice on "universal concern plus presence" jurisdiction is not yet substantial so as to afford the finding of a customary international law rule in its favor. Treaty practice providing for "universal concern plus treaty, presence and intra-regime territoriality or nationality jurisdiction" or "universal concern plus treaty and presence jurisdiction" is limited to the particular treaty regime only. In the light of this state of affairs, the possible application of the *Lotus* dictum and the presence requirement—especially the weak, procedural view of it—can be of significance and deserves attention.

58. The movement for "pure universal jurisdiction" has been "trending

down" since the conspicuous silence of the ICJ on the legitimacy of that jurisdiction in the *Arrest Warrant* case in 2002, when the Joint Separate Opinion of Judge Higgins, et al. found some evolutionary trend toward universal jurisdiction. [90] The subsequent downtrend may have been in no small measure due to the cautious Judgment in that case. That Judgment can be said to have, in an ingenious way, helped to inject some calming elements back into international relations. [91] With Belgium and Spain now having abandoned pure universal jurisdiction by narrowing down their statutes, the universal jurisdiction movement appears to be a moving train without its locomotive. [92]

## Postscript

The paper as originally published contains this long abstract:

The debates in the UNGA since 2009 on universal jurisdiction reveal great confusion on its concept, scope and application. True or pure universal jurisdiction is jurisdiction solely based on the universal concern character of the crime in issue. The concept and logic of universal jurisdiction is

---

[90]  Joint Separate Opinion, n. 17 above, paras. 45-52.

[91]  For a stronger assessment of the influence of the Arrest Warrant Judgment, see Alain Pellet, n. 66 above.

[92]  PS. : Since this paper was first published in 2011, pure universal jurisdiction has continued to be trending down, which led a commentator to observing a regime shift: Maximo Langer, Universal Jurisdiction is Not Disappearing: The Shift from 'Global Enforcer' to 'No Safe Haven' Universal Jurisdiction, 13 J. Int'l Crim. Justice ( 2015), 245 – 256. Recently, Argentina alone bucks the trend and exhibits some radical tendencies in this regard, difficult to assess now, without a clear domestic legal basis. Cf. María M. Márquez Velásquez, "The Argentinian Exercise of Universal Jurisdiction 12 Years After its Opening," Opinio Juris, February 4, 2022, https://opiniojuris.org/2022/02/04/the-argentinian-exercise-of-universal-jurisdiction-12-years-after-its-opening/.

understandable, as each State has an interest in matters of universal concern. Universal jurisdiction can be a powerful instrument for the international system to protect its interests and to protect human rights and fight against impunity. However, the exercise of universal jurisdiction by one State may infringe the sovereignty and sovereign equality of another State and can be abused, thus destabilizing international relations. These pros and cons and other factors have influenced the international law formation process in such a way that so far only universal jurisdiction over piracy has been accepted in international law in its favor. There is no "pure universal concern jurisdiction" over other crimes yet. The evidence of State practice on "universal concern plus presence" jurisdiction is not yet substantial so as to afford the finding of a customary international law rule. Treaty practice providing for "universal concern plus treaty, presence and intra-regime territoriality or nationality jurisdiction" or "universal concern plus treaty and presence jurisdiction" is limited to the particular treaty regime only. In the light of this state of affairs, the possible application of the *Lotus* dictum and the presence requirement—especially the weak, procedural view of it—can be of significance and deserves attention. The movement for "pure universal jurisdiction" has been "trending down" since the conspicuous silence on the legitimacy of universal jurisdiction in the *Arrest Warrant* case decided by the ICJ in 2002. The subsequent downtrend may have been in no small measure due to the cautious Judgment in that case. That Judgment can be said to have, in an ingenious way, helped to inject some calming elements back into international relations. With Belgium and Spain now having abandoned pure universal jurisdiction by narrowing down their statutes, the universal jurisdiction movement appears to be a moving train without its locomotive.